An Approach to Quantifying Desired Forest Conditions at Valley Forge National Historical Park

Technical Report NPS/NER/NRTR—2007/082

Ery Largay and Lesley A. Sneddon

NatureServe
11 Avenue de Lafayette, 5th Floor
Boston, MA 02111

March 2007

U.S. Department of the Interior
National Park Service
Northeast Region
Philadelphia, Pennsylvania

The Northeast Region of the National Park Service (NPS) comprises national parks and related areas in 13 New England and Mid-Atlantic states. The diversity of parks and their resources are reflected in their designations as national parks, seashores, historic sites, recreation areas, military parks, memorials, and rivers and trails. Biological, physical, and social science research results, natural resource inventory and monitoring data, scientific literature reviews, bibliographies, and proceedings of technical workshops and conferences related to these park units are disseminated through the NPS/NER Technical Report (NRTR) and Natural Resources Report (NRR) series. The reports are a continuation of series with previous acronyms of NPS/PHSO, NPS/MAR, NPS/BSO-RNR, and NPS/NERBOST. Individual parks may also disseminate information through their own report series.

Natural Resources Reports are the designated medium for information on technologies and resource management methods; "how to" resource management papers; proceedings of resource management workshops or conferences; and natural resource program descriptions and resource action plans.

Technical Reports are the designated medium for initially disseminating data and results of biological, physical, and social science research that addresses natural resource management issues; natural resource inventories and monitoring activities; scientific literature reviews; bibliographies; and peer-reviewed proceedings of technical workshops, conferences, or symposia.

Mention of trade names or commercial products does not constitute endorsement or recommendation for use by the National Park Service.

This report was accomplished under Cooperative Agreement 4560-B-0009, Supplemental Agreement No. 016, with assistance from the NPS. The statements, findings, conclusions, recommendations, and data in this report are solely those of the author(s), and do not necessarily reflect the views of the U.S. Department of the Interior, National Park Service.

Print copies of reports in these series, produced in limited quantity and only available as long as the supply lasts, or preferably, file copies on CD, may be obtained by sending a request to the address on the back cover. Print copies also may be requested from the NPS Technical Information Center (TIC), Denver Service Center, PO Box 25287, Denver, CO 80225-0287. A copy charge may be involved. To order from TIC, refer to document D-094.

This report may also be available as a downloadable portable document format file from the Internet at http://www.nps.gov/nero/science/.

Please cite this publication as:

Largay, E., and L. A. Sneddon. 2007. An approach to quantifying desired forest conditions at Valley Forge National Park. Technical Report NPS/NER/NRTR—2007/082. National Park Service. Philadelphia, PA.

NPS D-094   March 2007

Table of Contents

Page

Figures v

Tables vii

Appendixes ix

Abstract xi

Executive Summary xiii

Acknowledgments xv

Introduction 1

    Purpose 1

    Scope and Need 2

    Objectives 2

    Time Periods and Report Terms 2

Site Description 5

    Regional Information 5

    Park-specific Information 5

Methods 13

    Defining Desired Conditions 13

    Defining Desired Stand and Landscape Metrics Using Ecological
    Integrity Scorecard Protocol 14

Results 15

    Historic Conditions 15

    Existing Valley Forge National Historical Park Forest Conditions 22

    Ecological Stressors in the Valley Forge National Historical Park
    Forests 27

Table of Contents (continued)

Page

    Potential Trajectory of Valley Forge National Historical Park Forests
    Assuming No Management Actions 28

    Desired Conditions 30

Discussion 51

    Management Implications for Valley Forge National Historical Park 51

    Recommendations for Future Projects 51

Conclusions 53

Literature Cited 55

Figures

Page

Figure 1. Locations of Dry Oak Forest and Successional Tuliptree Forest at Valley Forge National Historical Park. 6

Figure 2. Dry Oak Forest at Valley Forge National Historical Park. 7

Figure 3. Dry Oak Forest (mesic variant) at Valley Forge National Historical Park. 8

Figure 4. Successional Tuliptree – Oak Forest at Valley Forge National Historical Park. 9

Figure 5. Bedrock geology of Valley Forge National Historical Park. 10

Figure 6. Proposed potential locations for target forest types of Dry Oak Forest, Dry-Mesic Chestnut Oak Forest, and Mesophyic Forest at Valley Forge National Historical Park. 31

Tables

                                                                                              Page

Table 1. Dates of historical terms used in this report. 3

Table 2. Tree taxa of 18th century southeastern Pennsylvania. 19

Table 3. Summary of target ecological integrity metrics compared to
existing forest conditions (where measured or known) for Valley Forge
National Historical Park Dry Oak Forests. 38

Table 4. Summary of target ecological integrity metrics compared to
existing forest condiions (where measured or known) for Valley Forge
National Historical Park Successional Tuliptree Forests. 48

Appendixes

                                                                       Page

Appendix A. NatureServe Ecological Classifications Glossary of Terms. 61

Appendix B. Draft Forest Condition Monitoring Protocol and Metrics. 71

Abstract

This report identifies an approach to quantifying desired conditions for two existing forest communities at Valley Forge National Historical Park (NHP); a Dry Oak Forest community and a Successional Tuliptree Forest community. The framework of the National Vegetation Classification System (NVCS) was used to write the descriptions for the desired conditions and compare target communities to globally described associations. We identified the desired condition of the Dry Oak Forest as a forest of essentially similar composition but with greater ecological integrity. The Successional Tuliptree Forest is itself an undesirable type, because as such, it has no known natural or historical analog. We propose that the desired condition of the Successional Tuliptree Forest is the conversion of this type to a native Mesophytic forest type with high ecological integrity. Historical records, witness tree data, and ecological studies from the Valley Forge area from the 1680–1800 time period were researched to determine the composition and structure of historical forests, particularly those that occurred on the landscape prior to and during the Revolutionary War encampment at Valley Forge from 1777–1778. We identified existing old growth examples of the Dry Oak Forest and the Mesophytic forest types as reference sites. Using a wide variety of historical data and present-day reference sites, we developed detailed descriptions of the target condition of both forest types.

Executive Summary

This report identifies one approach to quantifying possible desired forest conditions using the National Vegetation Classification System (NVCS) and ecological integrity criteria for two matrix forest communities at Valley Forge National Historical Park (NHP), a Dry Oak Forest type and a Successional Tuliptree Forest type. The target desired conditions were identified as historical forests that occurred on the Valley Forge landscape during the period of early European settlement of southeastern Pennsylvania prior to and during the Continental Army encampment period at Valley Forge NHP from 1777–1778. The time period for historical forest research was selected to complement the Valley Forge NHP's Draft General Management Plan Park Mission to preserve the natural and cultural resources that commemorate the encampment.

Descriptions of target communities were developed from witness tree data, historical accounts, past land use studies, and ecological studies that referenced the forests of the Valley Forge area. Research was also conducted on pre-European settlement forests to determine the historical composition of American chestnut (*Castanea dentata*) and to identify the disturbance regimes that maintained forests prior to European settlement. References to the landscape after encampment and through the 1900s were also reviewed to provide clues as to how early forests changed in the Valley Forge area.

The target forest types identified in this report include:

- A high-quality Dry Oak Forest community dominated by chestnut oak (*Quercus prinus*), black oak (*Quercus velutina*), and American chestnut (*Castanea dentata*) occurring on dry, acidic soils on steep slopes.

- Dry-Mesic Chestnut Oak Forest dominated by chestnut oak and northern red oak (*Quercus rubra*) occurring on moderate lower slopes with mesic soils.

- Mesophytic forest community dominated by an admixture of trees including oaks, especially white oak (*Quercus alba*), American beech (*Fagus grandifolia*), tuliptree (*Liriodendron tulipifera*), and hickories (*Carya* spp.) occurring on historically farmed, fertile, limestone-derived soils that support the existing Successional Tuliptree Forest.

Existing old growth examples of Dry Oak Forest and Mesophytic forest communities within the same ecoregion and with comparable vegetation composition, soil, and geological attributes were identified as reference sites. Target forest condition criteria, including stand-specific and landscape-level metrics, were identified from old-growth studies to provide quantitative stand-level data. These metrics can be used to guide restoration and for forest monitoring and management.

White-tailed deer (*Odocoilus virginianus*), exotic invasive plants, a lack of natural and anthropogenic stand-maintaining disturbance regimes, gypsy moth (*Lymantria dispar*) outbreaks, and abiotic factors such as surrounding land use are among some of the stressors influencing the ecological integrity of the existing Valley Forge NHP forests. Without some form of adaptive management to address the stressors or the impacts of these stressors, the existing Valley Forge

NHP forests are likely to be on successional trajectories with little ecological or historical value. This report proposes a set of desired conditions and potential target stand metrics for forest communities at Valley Forge NHP.

Acknowledgments

We extend our thanks to the many people who provided their time and assistance with this project. John Karish and Elizabeth Johnson of the Northeast Region of the National Park Service (NPS) provided funding and guidance. Kristina Heister, Deirdre Gibson, and Meghan Carfioli of Valley Forge National Historical Park provided us with previous research, expertise on ongoing management practices at the park, and comments on report drafts. Greg Podniesinski and Stephanie Perles of the Pennsylvania Natural Heritage Program and Jim Comiskey of the Mid-Atlantic Network of the NPS provided guidance and comments. Rickie White, Don Faber-Langendoen, and Judy Teague from NatureServe reviewed and commented on earlier drafts of this report.

David Orwig at Harvard Forest provided advice and guidance on eastern, old-growth, Dry Oak Forests and witness tree research. Brian Underwood at State University of New York provided useful comments on an early draft. Anne Rhoads at the University of Pennsylvania identified and described a number of old-growth sites in southeastern Pennsylvania that were cited in this report. Richard Lathrop and Ted Stiles at Rutgers University provided information on Helyar and Hutcheson Memorial Forests, two old-growth sites on the Rutgers University campus. John Nystedt and Janet Goehner-Jacobs at Saddler's Woods Conservation Association provided information on the old-growth stand at Saddler's Woods in Camden County, NJ. David Robertson at the Pennypack Ecological Restoration Trust provided detailed ecological information on the Peak Forest, an old-growth site in Huntington Valley, PA. The contributions and cooperation of all these individuals are greatly appreciated.

Introduction

Purpose

A vegetation map of Valley Forge National Historical Park using the National Vegetation Classification System (NVCS) was completed by ecologists from the Pennsylvania Natural Heritage Program and NatureServe in 2005 (Podniesinski et al. 2005). The map portrays the vegetation as it exists now, most of which has been substantially altered by human activity. Much of the vegetation in the park has been completely converted from the natural forested state to open fields and grasslands. The remaining "semi-natural" vegetation types have been degraded by invasive plants, browsing by deer (*Odocoilus virginianus*), and limited regeneration. Disturbance regimes have shifted since European settlement from natural processes such as fire and storm-induced canopy gaps, to extensive logging, and then to fire suppression. This shift in disturbance regimes and anthropogenic influences has set the existing forests on inevitably different successional pathways from those of the historical Valley Forge forests present prior to encampment in 1777–1778. Without management, it is likely that the forests will continue to degrade.

If the decision is made to attempt restoration of the Valley Forge National Historical Park (NHP) forests, what is the desired condition of those forests? In exploring this question, the Northeast Regional Office of the National Park Service (NPS) requested that NatureServe identify, describe, and quantify high-quality conditions of two forest types occurring at the park, the Dry Oak community (NVC type *Quercus prinus - Quercus (rubra, velutina) / Vaccinium angustifolium* Forest)[1] and the Successional Tuliptree community (NVC type *Liriodendron tulipifera - Quercus* spp. Forest).

NPS and NatureServe personnel collaborated during the proposal phase of this report and together identified pre-settlement conditions as a possible desired condition for both forest types. These early colonial settlement period (1680–1777) forest conditions were selected because they either were primary forests that had not been cleared or were late-stage secondary forests that closely resembled the composition of pre-European settlement forests. As such, they are considered to have high ecological integrity because they have not been altered in structure or composition by human activity. The ecological integrity of a community is a measure of the structure, composition, and function of a community as compared to a pristine or benchmark community operating within the bounds of natural or historic disturbance regimes (Lindenmayer and Franklin 2002; Tierney and Faber-Langendoen 2005). An "A" level occurrence represents the ecological integrity level closest to pristine or benchmark conditions. Ecological integrity criteria are generally developed for four levels, ranging from "A" (pristine) to "D" (poor). Although "A" is the ideal condition, in practice, a "B" or even a "C" level may be selected as the most achievable goal, given the constraints imposed by funding, personnel, time, landscape context, and other factors. In this report, we provide "A" level criteria because it is necessary to

---

[1] Since completion of the Valley Forge National Historical Park vegetation map, re-evaluation of lower slope plots originally assigned to the Dry Oak Forest at the park may be more appropriately assigned to the Dry-Mesic Chestnut Oak Forest (*Quercus prinus - Quercus rubra / Hamamelis virginiana* Forest). A description of this type is provided, but development of detailed metrics was beyond the scope of this project.

1

have a vision of the pristine condition in order to develop criteria at lower, but more achievable interim levels. Development of "B," "C," and "D" conditions were beyond the scope of this project.

Scope and Need

The scope of this project was to identify two target forest communities for the existing Dry Oak and Successional Tuliptree forest communities; amass existing information for both forest types; analyze deer exclosure data to identify herbaceous and shrub species suppressed by heavy deer browse; research American chestnut target composition; describe target vegetation structure and compositions; describe target environmental (vegetation habitat) condition (soil, coarse woody debris, microtopography); and describe the landscape context for these two Valley Forge NHP forest types.

The mission of Valley Forge NHP is to "preserve the cultural and natural resources that commemorate the encampment of the Continental Army at Valley Forge in 1777–78" (Valley Forge NHP 2006). The National Park Service Management Policies (2001) permit the intervention in natural biological or physical processes "to restore natural ecosystem functioning that has been disrupted by past or ongoing human activities." The two directives pose a challenging task that requires finding a suitable balance between the natural and the historical landscape. This report is intended to provide the information necessary to make informed decisions to achieve that balance.

Objectives

The objective of this report is provide detailed information on the desired structure, composition, habitat, and landscape context of two forest types occurring at Valley Forge NHP. Our goal was to compile and analyze data from a wide range of sources, including historical records, pollen analyses, witness tree data, naturalist descriptions, ecological studies, and existing vegetation data from the park, as well as to identify old-growth stands as reference sites within the same ecoregion that exhibit species and an environmental setting similar to the target types. Through analysis of these data, we propose target or "A" level stand and landscape level metrics for both forest types for use in ecological integrity assessments and forest monitoring and management. It is important to note that our objective is not to advocate restoration of pre-settlement forests at Valley Forge NHP. Rather, our goal is to provide detailed information that can be used to guide restoration should that course of action be selected.

Time Periods and Report Terms

This report references a number of time periods in Pennsylvania history. Table 1 identifies the time periods referenced in the report and the range of dates the time period encompasses. Appendix A contains a glossary of terms used throughout this report.

Table 1. Dates of historical terms used in this report.

Time Period Referenced	Dates
Pre-European settlement of Valley Forge area	before 1680
Early colonial settlement of Valley Forge	1680–1800
Revolutionary War Valley Forge encampment	1777–1778
Post encampment	after 1779

Regional Information

Valley Forge NHP is located in Chester and Montgomery counties, within the Upland Piedmont Plateau ecological region in southeastern Pennsylvania (Keys et al. 1995). The park consists of 1,403 ha (3,466 ac). It is located just south of Braun's (1950) boundary between the Glaciated and Piedmont Sections of the Oak-Chestnut Forest Region, which also approximates the boundary between the Lowland and Upland U.S. Forest Service subsections of the Piedmont (Kasmer et al. 1994; Keys et al. 1995). The area has a long history of human impacts from forest clearing for encampment during the Revolutionary War (1777–1778), agriculture, industrial use, and development. All of these factors, in addition to the bedrock geology, soil composition, and site-specific characteristics, such as slope, aspect, and moisture regime, influence the current-day vegetation patterns at Valley Forge NHP (Podniesinski et al. 2005).

Park-specific Information

<u>Vegetation</u>

The predominant existing forest communities at Valley Forge NHP include a Dry Oak Forest that occurs primarily on ridges and slopes of Mount Misery and Mount Joy, and a Successional Tuliptree Forest that occurs on lower slopes and flat terrain (Figure 1). The Dry Oak community covers approximately 158 ha (390 ac) and the Successional Tuliptree community covers approximately 151 ha (374 ac) of the park (Davis et al. 2006).

The Dry Oak Forest type is most common on the slopes of Mount Joy and Mount Misery within the park (Figure 2). The canopy is dominated by drought-tolerant chestnut oak and black oak with blackgum (*Nyssa sylvatica*) and scarlet oak (*Quercus coccinea*) as occasional codominants. The subcanopy is characterized by moderate to dense cover of blackgum, red maple (*Acer rubrum*), and sassafras (*Sassafras albidum*). The tall shrub layer is often diagnostic for this type, characterized by moderate to dense cover of mountain laurel (*Kalmia latifolia*). In some stands, the tall-shrub layer is dominated by young blackgum. Also common in the tall-shrub layer are red maple, sassafras, and witch-hazel (*Hamamelis virginiana*). The low-shrub and herbaceous layers are typically very sparse or absent, presumably due to heavy deer browse. The low-shrub layer, when present, is limited to seedlings of canopy trees and a few ericaceous species: early lowbush blueberry (*Vaccinium pallidum*), black huckleberry (*Gaylussacia baccata*), and pink azalea (*Rhododendron periclymenoides*). Herbaceous plants typically occur as solitary individuals or small clumps, when present. Common herbaceous species include striped pipsissewa (*Chimaphila maculata*), hay-scented fern (*Dennstaedtia punctilobula*), marginal woodfern (*Dryopteris marginalis*), and Indian cucumber-root (*Medeola virginiana*).

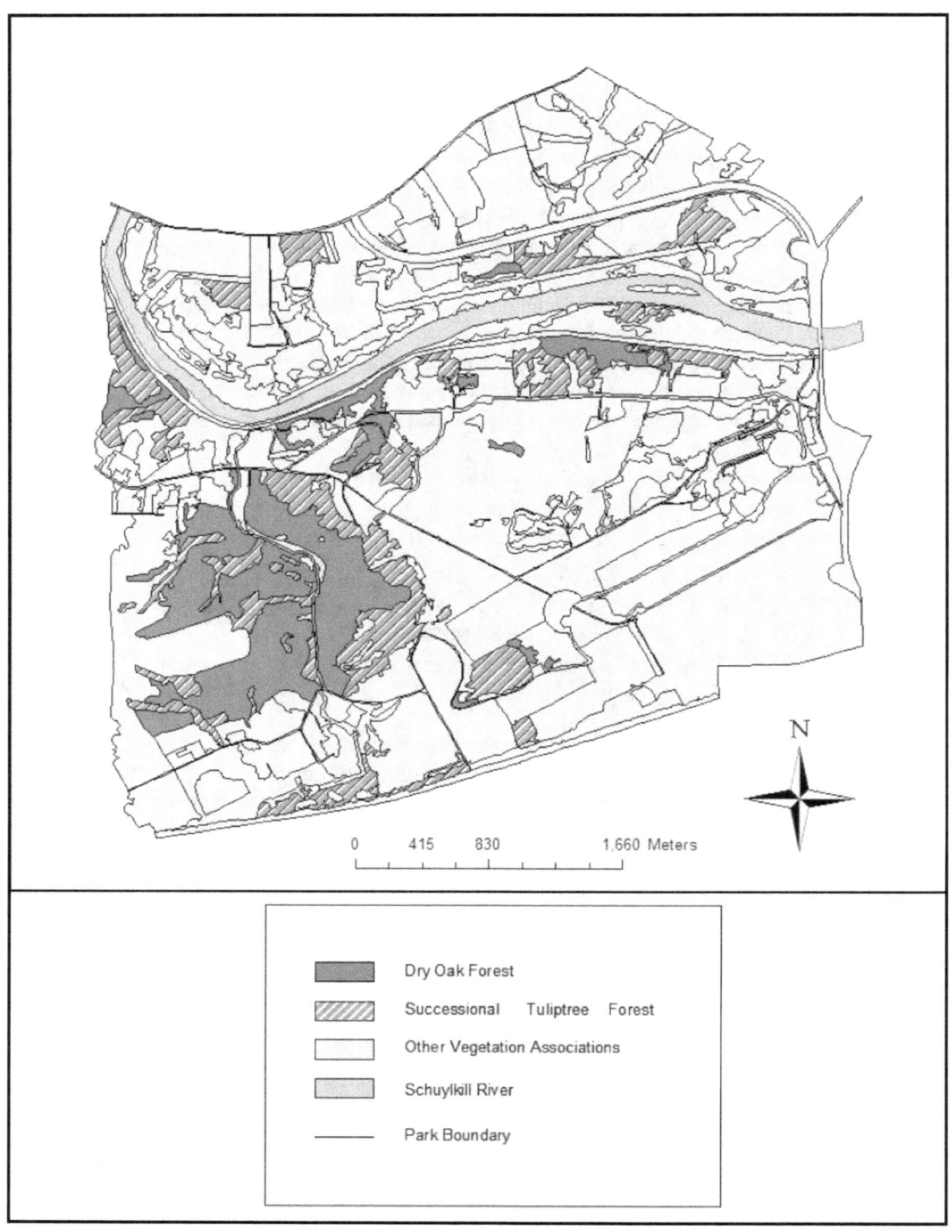

Figure 1. Locations of Dry Oak Forest and Successional Tuliptree Forest at Valley Forge National Historical Park (adapted from Podniesinski et al. 2005).

Figure 2. Dry Oak Forest at Valley Forge National Historical Park. April 2002. NAD 1983 / UTM easting 460723, northing 4437578 (from Podniesinski et al. 2005).

The mesic variant[2] of the Dry Oak Forest (Podniesinski et al. 2005) occurs on moderate slopes with slightly more mesic soils than is found on the upper slopes (Figure 3). Canopy dominants are dry-site oaks (chestnut oak, black oak, and scarlet oak), but the canopy also includes a greater proportion of other hardwood species, including white oak, red maple, tuliptree, American beech, and sassafras. A subcanopy is usually present, characterized by a mix of hardwood species such as red maple, sassafras, American beech, chestnut oak, and black oak. Typical tall shrubs include flowering dogwood, witch-hazel, and mountain laurel. The tall-shrub layer varies from sparse to abundant, with flowering dogwood (*Cornus florida*) exceeding 50% cover in some locations. The low-shrub and herbaceous layers are very sparse to nearly absent, presumably the result of intense deer browse. The low-shrub layer is characterized by seedlings of the canopy and subcanopy woody species. Typical herbaceous species include garlic mustard (*Alliaria petiolata*), Japanese stiltgrass (*Microstegium vimineum*), and Pennsylvania sedge (*Carex pensylvanica*).

---

[2] This variant may be classified as a separate NVC association in future analyses.

Figure 3. Dry Oak Forest (mesic variant) at Valley Forge National Historical Park. April 2002. NAD 1983 / UTM easting 462193, northing 4440211 (from Podniesinski et al. 2005).

The Successional Tuliptree community occurs throughout the park on a variety of substrates and soil types. This type occurs as mid-successional and mature forest stands. Some of these stands were planted 70 to 80 years ago. The most characteristic feature of this community type is the dominance of tuliptree (Figure 4). Tuliptree is the only dominant in many stands, with black oak and white ash (*Fraxinus americana*) codominant or subdominant in others. Other occasional canopy trees include red maple, northern red oak, and sassafras. The subcanopy is usually open (typically less than 30% total cover, though may approach 50%), characterized by tuliptree, red maple, tall individuals of flowering dogwood, blackgum, occasional redbud (*Cercis canadensis*), and sassafras. The shrub layer is also open and appears to be pruned below 1.5 m (5 ft) by heavy deer browse. Typical shrub species are flowering dogwood (clear dominant in the shrub layer), northern spicebush (*Lindera benzoin*), mountain laurel, and the nonnative Japanese honeysuckle (*Lonicera japonica*). Smooth blackhaw (*Viburnum prunifolium*) also occurs sporadically. The herbaceous layer has very low diversity and is dominated by exotics, including Japanese stiltgrass, except in stands with a very dense canopy, in which case there may be a high proportion of bare ground. Other herbaceous associates in addition to Japanese stiltgrass include garlic mustard, Oriental lady's-thumb (*Polygonum caespitosum*), jack-in-the-pulpit (*Arisaema triphyllum*), and Canadian clearweed (*Pilea pumila*). Characteristic species that occur in the Successional Tuliptree Forest community, and that do not typically occur in the oak forests, include hairy Solomon's-seal (*Polygonatum pubescens*), Maryland black snakeroot (*Sanicula marilandica*), and alpine enchanter's nightshade (*Circaea alpina*).

Figure 4. Successional Tuliptree – Oak Forest at Valley Forge National Historical Park. April 2002. NAD 1983 / UTM easting 461597, northing 4437980 (from Podniesinski et al. 2005).

Substrate

One of the clues to identifying past forest types is to understand the underlying bedrock throughout the park, as some tree species and forest communities are preferential to certain soil and bedrock types, while others have more general requirements. Four primary types of bedrock occur at Valley Forge NHP (Figure 5).

The Triassic Age Stockton Formation (Trs), consisting of sandstone, siltstone, and mudstone, covers the entire portion of the park north of the Schuylkill River and a narrow band adjacent to the south side of the river. The topography associated with the Stockton Formation is that of low rolling hills north of the river and generally north-facing slopes south of the river. Floodplain forests and successional forests are predominant on these soils at Valley Forge NHP.

The Cambrian Ledger Formation (Cl), made up of dolostone and limestone, occurs as a valley within the southern and southwestern portions of the park. Both limestone and dolostone are carbonate rocks. Dolostone is a made up of dolomite, which consists of calcium and magnesium carbonate. Soils formed from these rocks are fertile and soluble. Limestone was reportedly mined from the Valley Forge area as early as 1783 and was used for fertilizer on fields and for refining iron ore (Rhoads et al. 1989). Dolostone was mined for magnesium in Valley Forge

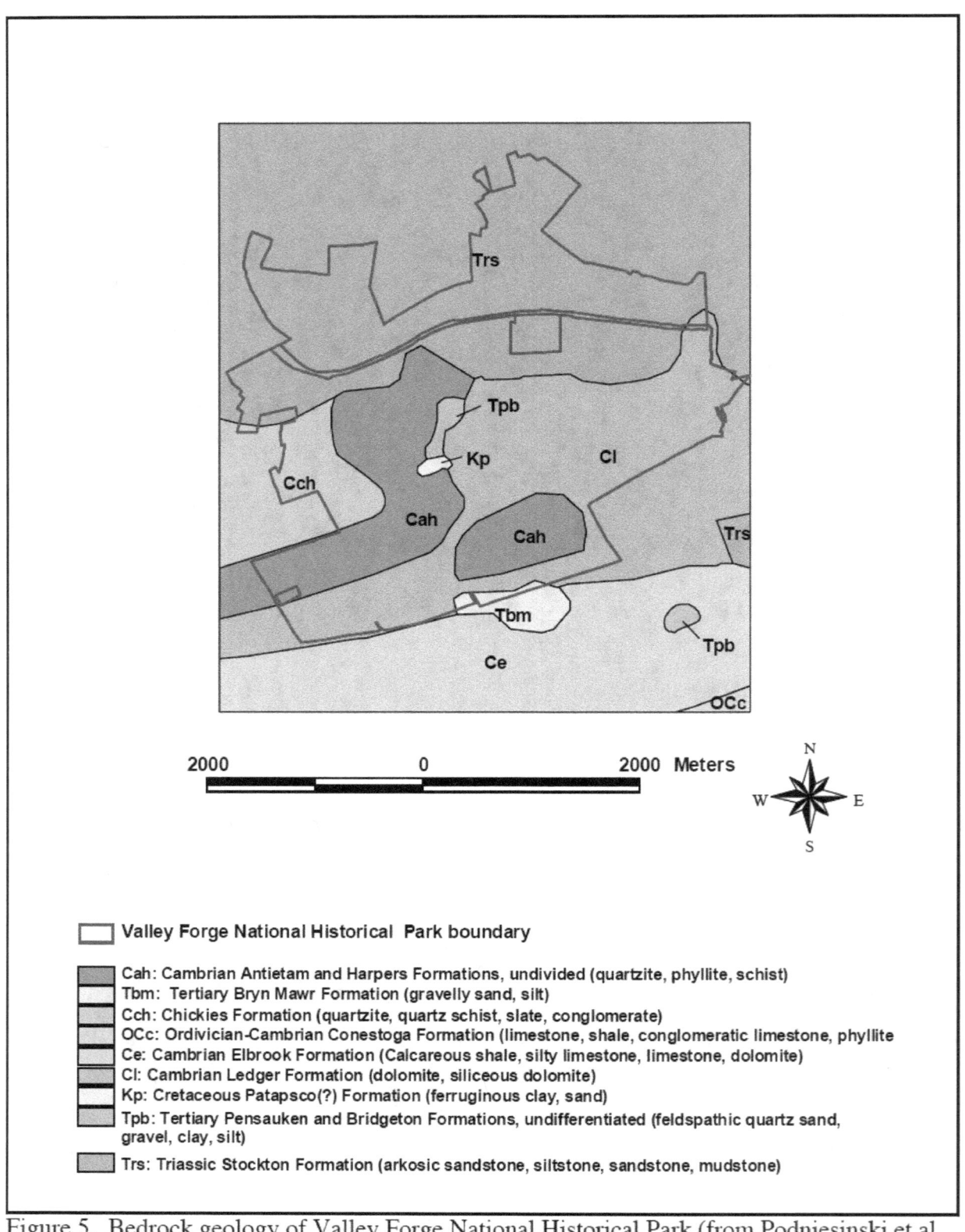

Figure 5. Bedrock geology of Valley Forge National Historical Park (from Podniesinski et al. 2005).

NHP in the 1970s. Caves and sinkholes occur within this substrate in the southern portion of the park (Pennsylvania Geological Survey 1993).

The fertile soils derived from areas overlying the Triassic Stockton and Cambrian Ledger Formations were farmed intensively for two hundred years (Rhoads et al. 1989; Black and Abrams 2001). The soils on the southeastern side of the Schuylkill River within the park are delineated as Class I or Class II soils for agriculture in the United States Department of Agriculture Soil Conservation Service (USDA SCS) Survey of Montgomery County (1967) and the primary soil type south of the Schuylkill River is Duffield (USDA SCS 1967; Davis et al. 2006). The existing forest communities occurring on these soils are successional and grew after field and farm abandonment.

On the west side of the park, Mount Misery consists of the Cambrian Age Chickies Formation (Cch), a very hard, erosion-resistant rock composed of quartzite and quartz schist. Dry Oak Forests dominated by chestnut oak, black oak, northern red oak, and white oak are common on these acidic, well-drained, rocky Edgemont soils occurring on upper slopes (USDA SCS 1967). The infertile soils and the steep terrain on Mount Misery were likely unsuitable for farming historically. The forests on this ridge were used as woodlots for charcoal production (Rhoads et al. 1989).

Mount Joy and Wayne's Woods occur on the slightly younger Cambrian Age Antietam and Harpers (undivided) Formations (Cah). These rock types are composed of quartzite, schist, and phyllite, and are fairly erosion resistant. Edgemont stony loam soils derived from these formations can be somewhat calcareous and are slightly more mesic than soils that occur on the Chickies Quartzite Formation (Pennsylvania Geological Survey 1981; Pennsylvania Bureau of Topographic and Geographic Survey 2001; Podniesinski et al. 2005). These moderate slopes may have been better suited for farming historically than the steeper slopes and rockier soils of Mount Misery (Rhoads et al. 1989). The Successional Tuliptree community is common on these substrates as well as those derived from the Triassic Stockton Formation.

Methods

Defining Desired Conditions

Forests in southeastern Pennsylvania were researched from the time period of 1640–1800 to identify forest communities that occurred on the Valley Forge NHP landscape historically, particularly during the period of the Revolutionary War encampment (1777–1778). Data sources included historical records, pollen analyses, witness tree data, naturalist descriptions, ecological studies, and existing vegetation data from the park. Historical documents, including letters, deeds, a bird census from 1901, witness tree data dating from 1700–1800, and a past land use study at the park, were reviewed for references to tree species and other vegetation on the landscape prior to and during the time of encampment.

Regional, county, town, and stand-level ecological studies, including pollen analyses, naturalist descriptions, and academic reports, were also reviewed. Bedrock geology, soil texture and type, and landscape position were also examined. The proportion of American chestnut in both target communities was estimated from pollen records and historical accounts of the species from the area.

More recent ecological studies completed at Valley Forge NHP were also reviewed. These studies included the Bowersox and Larrick (1999) Long-term Vegetation Monitoring report, a deer exclosure study conducted by Heister et al. (2002), and the Podniesinski et al. (2005) Vegetation Classification and Mapping report for Valley Forge NHP prepared by the Pennsylvania Natural Heritage Program and NatureServe. Some predictions for future forest conditions in the absence of management were estimated using data from these sources. These data were also used where applicable to qualitatively assess the current composition and integrity of the Dry Oak and Successional Tuliptree communities.

Once target communities were identified from this research, descriptions were developed for the communities and compared to corresponding associations in the National Vegetation Classification (NVC)[3]. The NVCS was adopted by the Federal Geographic Data Committee (FGDC) as the reporting standard for all federal agencies to promote sharing vegetation information and reporting national statistics. Use of a nationally standardized classification allows for the comparison of vegetation types across political, jurisdictional, and geographic boundaries. The USGS–NPS vegetation mapping program is based on the NVCS, ensuring that the same set of units are used to map and describe all vegetation types across all parks.

Old-growth reference sites supporting similar vegetation as the target forest types were identified from the literature and from personal communications with experts in the field. Sites were selected based on having similar species composition and structure and similar environmental conditions, including geology, soil composition, moisture regime, and ecoregional location as the described target communities.

---

[3] The NVC (National Vegetation Classification) is the set of classification units within the organizational scheme of the NVCS (National Vegetation Classification System).

Defining Desired Stand and Landscape Metrics Using Ecological Integrity Scorecard Protocol

Desired ("A" level) stand and landscape metrics were identified using the Draft Forest Condition Monitoring Protocols developed by Tierney and Faber-Langendoen (2005) for the NPS Northeast Temperate Network (NETN). These protocols were developed by NETN park staff and managers, academic and government scientists, NatureServe ecologists, and other land management stakeholders to identify indicators of ecological condition. The protocols identify stand-specific and landscape-level metrics that can be measured to monitor forest stands over long periods of time (Appendix B). Ecological integrity is assessed using these metrics by comparing key elements of the structure, composition, and function of a forest community to the same elements of a reference area or to historical measurements of the same stand.

Although the protocols were recently developed, they were selected for application in this report because it is likely they will form the basis for future forest monitoring by the Mid-Atlantic Vital Signs Network and other networks, including the Eastern Rivers and Mountain Network and the National Capital Region Network (NPS, Comiskey, Mid-Atlantic Network Coordinator, conversation, Aug. 15, 2006). Therefore, linking the desired condition of Valley Forge NHP forests to this framework will help translate monitoring results to management decisions. The metrics serve an important foundation since these thresholds can be modified and adjusted as the forests are monitored and more is learned about their structure, composition, and dynamics (NPS, Comiskey, Mid-Atlantic Network Coordinator, conversation, Aug. 15, 2006).

Results

Historic Conditions

Pre-European Settlement Forests Prior to Encampment (1640–1777)

The ridge tops of Mount Misery and Mount Joy likely have always supported a Dry Oak Forest; however, the composition has changed over time due to various disturbances. Frelich and Reich (2002, p. 117) reported that in chestnut oak forests "standwide disturbances occurred approximately every 21 years during presettlement times (prior to 1775) and were reduced during heavy Euro-American exploitation (1775–1900) to every 31 years in modern times (after 1900); in addition, the mode of disturbance shifted from mainly natural (wind and fire) to anthropogenic forces (intense harvesting for charcoal production), based on the historical record. The reduction of harvesting and fire events coupled with the eradication of American chestnut by blight this century have allowed these coppice stands to mature into oak-dominated forests that exist today." The eastern face of Mount Joy and most of Wayne's Woods have gentler slopes and less droughty soils than do the western and northern slopes and likely supported the Dry-Mesic Chestnut Oak Forest variant of the Dry Oak Forest (now recognized as a separate association in the NVC) prior to clearing at the time of encampment at Valley Forge in 1777–1778 (Podniesinski et al. 2005).

Mesophytic forests, also known historically as "rich woods" where oaks shared dominance with American beech, hickories, tuliptree, American chestnut, white ash, and possibly small amounts of sugar maple (*Acer saccharum*), may have once occurred on limestone derived soils associated with the Stockton and Ledger Formations prior to forest clearing (Harshberger 1904; Gordon 1941; Podniesinski et al. 2005). This forest type was also historically reported to occur adjacent to rivers and creeks. Kasmer et al. (1984) found American beech as a codominant or dominant in the forest canopy on Stockton soils in 12 of 15 stands they sampled in the Piedmont Lowlands. American beech-dominated stands typically occurred on sheltered north slopes and ravines (naturally occurring fire breaks); while mixed oaks and hickories dominated on south-facing slopes (Harshberger 1919; Gordon 1941; Braun 1950).

Rhoads et al. (1989) indicated that 60% of the Valley Forge NHP area was forested in the mid-1760s,, declining to 30% by 1777. It is possible that at the time of encampment some of the remaining forests at Valley Forge NHP had not been logged. Portions of the Dry Oak Forests occurring on the relatively inaccessible crests and steep slopes of Mount Misery and Mount Joy may have remained untouched in favor of the easily logged areas currently supporting Successional Tuliptree Forests, which were most likely cleared prior to encampment due to their occurrence on flat, fertile soils. It is possible that small remnants of a Mesophytic forest remained during encampment, as suggested by witness tree data. During and after encampment the literature documents widespread clearing of forests for fuelwood, fenceposts, rails, and building materials (Rhoads et al. 1989). Although many forests occurring at the time of encampment were largely 100-year-old secondary forests, they reflected the character of the primary forests that occurred on the landscape in Pennsylvania in the 1680s (Gordon 1941).

We conducted a review of many paleoecological records and studies to determine the potential composition of pre-encampment Valley Forge NHP forest communities. Prior to European settlement and certainly before encampment, forests of acidic shallow soils of crests and steep slopes were most likely dominated by white oak, black oak, northern red oak, chestnut oak, scarlet oak, and American chestnut. A mesophytic forest characterized by oaks, American beech, tuliptree, and hickories likely occurred on gentle north-facing slopes or sheltered areas protected from fire and on fertile soils derived from dolostone and limestone. These forests may also have occurred on soils derived from mudstone, sandstone, and shale adjacent to the Schuylkill River (Braun 1950; Dey 2002).

The composition and structure of forests from the pre-European settlement period were maintained by natural disturbances such as lightning fire and drought as well as anthropogenic disturbances including Native American fires. Paleobotanical studies of microfossils (pollen and air-borne charcoal) provide evidence of past fires. These deposits date natural and anthropogenic fires that influenced pre-European settlement forest composition. Native Americans set periodic low-intensity ground fires for a number of reasons—to promote nut and fruit production by oak and American chestnut trees, to clear the understory to facilitate hunting of wildlife, to clear forests for maize cultivation, and for the creation of small settlements. The fire regime created a mosaic of small patches within the forested landscape, as areas burned for maize and settlements were relatively small in size (Frelich and Reich 1996; White and White 1996; Dey 2002; Foster et al. 2002; McCarthy 2003). Native American fires and natural lightning-induced fires, in combination with a warm and dry climate, maintained the stability of pre-European settlement forests dominated by oaks and American chestnut throughout the Holocene (Foster et al. 2002). Fires eliminated or reduced competition from shade-tolerant understory species such as American beech and fire-sensitive maples. The understory was open due to the periodic surface fires, with occasional scattered shrubs (Frelich and Reich 1996; Abrams 2002; Dey 2002). Although some Valley Forge NHP forests have this same open and park-like look today, heavy deer browse and a high incidence of nonnative plants, rather than surface fires, maintain the present forest structure and composition.

Oak - chestnut forests dominated the region south of the glacial boundary in the Piedmont ecoregion (Braun 1950; Buell et al. 1966) prior to European settlement, throughout early colonial settlement of the area, and up until the early 1900s. The location of Valley Forge NHP south of the glacial boundary in the Uplands section of the Piedmont suggests that forests characterized by oaks and American chestnut, with lesser amounts of hickory, dominated the forest canopy, rather than the mesophytic forests that occurred more prominently north of the glacial boundary in New Jersey (Braun 1950; Keever 1973; Kasmer et al. 1994). Sugar maple was uncommon in these forests. In Bucks County, Pennsylvania, just to the northeast of Chester County, however, sugar maple is more common (Kasmer et al. 1994).

Gordon (1941) referenced a description of vegetation we classify as the Dry Oak community from Darlington's 1826 flora of the West Chester area. Darlington described the original forest of Penn's Woods from 1680, prior to clearing, as having original forest indicators adapted to acidic sites: chestnut oak, black oak, black birch, and sassafras. He noted that American beech was absent in dominant stands, although suppressed American beech could occur in the understory. Flowering dogwood was most abundant in the shrub layer, while heaths including mountain laurel, wintergreen, and striped pipsissewa were scattered in the lower shrub layers.

Overlease (1987) also described a "hypothesized original xeric forest community" dominated by black oak, scarlet oak, chestnut oak, white oak, northern red oak, tuliptree, American chestnut, and American beech, with red maple, blackgum, and flowering dogwood common in the understory. In his description, mapleleaf viburnum, mountain laurel, and blueberries dominate the shrub layer, and the herb layer is inconspicuous. The existing Dry Oak Forest at Valley Forge NHP is very likely to be the same vegetation type described by Gordon, Darlington, and Overlease above. This forest type was historically cut over multiple times for charcoal and was not used for agriculture (Podniesinski et al. 2005).

Braun (1950) indicated that small pockets of mesophytic forest most likely occurred in the northern part of the Piedmont in Pennsylvania. She attributed their occurrence to a "small eastern refugium of mixed Tertiary forest not reached by Pleistocene ice, but isolated from the main area of that forest on the Appalachian Plateau and deprived of some of its species because of glacial ice and lack of suitable edaphic environments adjacent to the south on which to expand (p. 512)."

Overlease (1987) also described a "hypothetical" mixed mesic forest in his studies within southeastern Pennsylvania. These forests were among the earliest to be cleared after European settlement in the late 1600s due to their occurrence on mesic soils that were suitable to farming and gentle slopes that were easily accessible. He depicted these pre-settlement mesic forests as dominated by black oak, white oak, northern red oak, American chestnut, white ash, tuliptree, pignut hickory, mockernut hickory, bitternut hickory (*Carya cordiformis*), and American beech. This forest community had a relatively open shrub layer, and noticeably less flowering dogwood.

Valley Forge National Historical Park Forests During and After Encampment (1777–1900)

Early Historical Accounts from Valley Forge NHP: Historical records, including letters from Valley Forge and a land use map from the time of encampment (Duportail map in Rhoads et al. 1989), provide descriptions of the forests and forest composition at the time of encampment. One letter from 1814 describes the change in timber species at Valley Forge in 1777: "the timber prevalent about Valley Forge, previously to its being fallen for the use of the American army, in the autumn of 1777, and winter and spring of 1778, consisted of white oak, black oak, Spanish oak (scarlet oak), rarely interspersed with scrubby American chestnut and hickory (Wayne 1814)." Wayne (1814) further described the ratio of hickory to American chestnut as 16:1 in areas where white oak, black oak, and scarlet oak formerly grew the previous year. Wayne (1814) wrote that, on soils selected by early farmers for agriculture, "the farmers, in many parts of this county, are so decidedly convinced of the change of timber, that they reluctantly cut their full grown white oak, black oak, and hickory; knowing that these species will be succeeded by some other, of a quality inferior for fuel." The reference to hickory on these sites cleared by farmers suggests the presence of a Mesophytic community supporting oaks and hickories at the time of encampment.

Rhoads et al. (1989) presented a land use map entitled "Duportail map." This map was made just prior to the encampment period from 1777–1778 and illustrates the locations of woodlands, wetlands, meadows with scattered trees, and orchards. Thirty-three percent of the Valley Forge NHP landscape was forested prior to encampment. These areas included the steep slopes and ridges of Mount Misery and Mount Joy, along Valley Creek, and the north-facing slopes on the south side of the Schuylkill River. All of these forested areas were most likely unsuitable for cultivation. The dominant forest species included oak, American chestnut, and hickory. Rhoads et al. (1989) suggested from their research that these woodlands were most likely in phases of early successional growth during encampment, as they were typically used as a source of wood by the troops. By the end of encampment, the forests were completely cleared and wood was described as scarce. In one letter from General Washington in December of 1777 it was recommended that the troops "in cutting their firewood...save such parts of each tree as will do for buildings, reserving 16 or 18 feet of each trunk for logs" (p. 68). Another letter from January 1778 indicated that there was "not a tree standing beyond Schuylkill nor in ye city" (p. 68). Stands used for charcoal were completely cleared, often at 25–30 year intervals (Mikan et al. 1994). In the 1800s woodlots were used for fence posts, rails, firewood, and building materials (Rhoads et al. 1989). The forests endured many generations of cutting and re-growth, which favored stump-sprouting species such as chestnut oak, black oak, and American chestnut (Overlease 1987; Podniesinski et al. 2005).

Witness Tree Data: At the time of encampment, white oak, black oak, northern red oak, chestnut oak, American chestnut, and hickory were the most commonly reported witness trees from the Valley Forge NHP area. They were also the most commonly reported species in the region as evidenced by witness tree data from Hopewell Furnace National Historic Site (NHS) and in the Piedmont Uplands of Lancaster County in Pennsylvania (Abrams 1992, 2003).

Rhoads et al. (1989) collected 84 citations of witness trees from Valley Forge NHP from the late 1700s deed descriptions of the encampment area to determine potential species composition of early forests. A similar tally of 513 witness trees from 1733–1794 was completed near the Hopewell Furnace NHS in Berks County, also in the Uplands Section of the Piedmont (Mikan et al. 1994). Likewise, Black and Abrams (2001) collected witness tree data on 4,754 trees recorded between 1735 and 1765 as occurring within the Piedmont Uplands subsection of Lancaster County in southeastern Pennsylvania (Table 2). These data support the hypothesis that a Dry Oak Forest and a Mesophytic forest existed historically in the Valley Forge area in the late 1700s, as many of the characteristic tree species from both communities were recorded as present on the landscape.

Black oak, white oak, scarlet oak, hickories, and American chestnut emerge as the most frequently recorded species in the 1700's. White oak represented 35–41% of witness trees in limestone valleys (in central Pennsylvania), but only 6%–13% on sandstone ridges which were dominated by pine (*Pinus* spp.), chestnut oak, and American chestnut (Abrams 2003). The successional trees we see today in abundance at Valley Forge NHP, including tuliptree, white ash, and red maple, are minor components in the witness tree records. This may be due to a surveyor bias for larger trees. White oak, for instance, was commonly cited in witness tree data, likely because it was a large diameter tree that typically grew on the flat, gentle terrain that was selected for settlement or agriculture (Abrams 2002). However, the abundance of oaks, hickories, and American chestnut in the 1700s is more likely a result of a historic fire regime, which favored them over the fire-intolerant and more successional species (Abrams 2003).

Table 2. Tree taxa of 18th century southeastern Pennsylvania.

Species	Valley Forge NHP[a] % Citations	Hopewell Furnace NHS[b] % Composition	Piedmont Uplands Lancaster County, PA[c] % Composition
hickory	26	14.6	11.8
black oak	16	33.1	24.2
white oak	14	16.6	26.6
oak	12	0.0	0.0
Spanish oak (=scarlet oak)	8	4.2	6.4
American chestnut	5	15.4	17.7
gum (=blackgum)	5	1.8	1.4
sugar (= sugar maple)	2	0.6	0.0
water beech (=American beech)	2	0.0	0.11
chestnut oak	1	6.8	6.0
elm	1	0.0	0.02
mulberry	1	0.0	0.0
sassafras	11	0.0	0.04
buttonwood	1	0.2	0.0
walnut	1	0.8	0.21
dogwood	1	0.0	0.04
apple	1	0.0	0.0
poplar (=tuliptree)	0	1.2	0.5
ash	0	1.0	0.34
birch	0	1.0	0.5
maple	0	1.0	2.0
ironwood	0	0.2	0.0

[a]percent of time cited in 98 late-1700's deed descriptions of Valley Forge NHP properties (Rhoads et al. 1989);
[b]percent composition of witness trees from the Hopewell Furnace NHS vicinity from 1733 to 1794 (Mikan et al.1994);
[c]percent composition of witness trees in the Piedmont Uplands of Lancaster County, PA from 1735–1765 (Black and Abrams 2001).

Later Historical Accounts of Valley Forge NHP: Later records from the turn of the twentieth century describe secondary forests where hickory, tuliptree, American beech, and red maple were canopy associates with white, black, and northern red oaks in what we interpret to be a mesic successional forest in Berwyn, Chester County (Unknown 1901). Flowering dogwood, mountain laurel, and spicebush are the predominant shrubs described, along with black walnut and slippery elm (*Ulmus rubra*)[4]. The author described a diverse herbaceous layer with species such as "the windflower (*Anemone* sp.), mandrake (*Podophyllum peltatum*), bloodroot, shepherds' purse (*Capsella bursa-pastoris*), pepper grass (*Lepidium* spp.), yellow violet (*Viola pubescens*), jewel weed (*Impatiens capensis*), poison ivy (*Toxicodendron radicans*), wild sarsaparilla (*Aralia nudicaulis*), bush honeysuckle (*Lonicera* sp.), partridgeberry (*Mitchella repens*), wild astor (sic.) (*Aster* sp.), wild huckleberry, trailing arbutus (*Epigea repens*), spotted prince's pine (sic.) (*Chimaphila umbellata*), pennyroyal (*Mentha pulegium*), boneset

---

[4] Plants were listed by common name only in the report – probable Latin names are suggested by the authors of this report, but caution should be used.

(*Eupatorium* spp.), Indian pipe (*Monotropa uniflora*), poke (*Phytolacca americana*), Indian turnip (*Arisaema triphyllum*), calamus (*Acorus calamus*), showy orchid (*Galearis spectabilis*), and winter, summer, and maiden hair ferns" (Unknown 1901).

This report is of interest for several reasons. First, very few historical accounts describe and identify herbaceous species. Also, some of the herbaceous species listed are generally characteristic of rich soils influenced by carbonate deposits such as limestone or dolostone and are more diverse compared to the inconspicuous herbaceous layer described in Dry Oak Forests by other authors. Some of these same herbaceous species were observed in the understory of the existing Successional Tuliptree community in the Valley Forge NHP fenced plots of the deer exclosure study and in the Valley Forge NHP vegetation mapping plots (Heister et al 2002; Podniesinski et al. 2005).

County floras, naturalist descriptions, and more recent ecological studies also provide some evidence of past forest composition. Valley Forge falls within Braun's (1950) American chestnut - Oak Forest region. Braun (1950) defined the Oak - Chestnut Forest Region by the characteristic presence of oak and American chestnut. She indicated that other oak, oak-chestnut, oak-chestnut-tuliptree and possibly mesophytic forests also occurred within the region based on site-specific conditions and physiography. She described forests that we interpret to be the Dry Oak community and the Mesophytic forest community occurring with the Piedmont Upland of southeastern Pennsylvania. Gordon (1941) described the placement of Chester County within in the Chestnut - Chestnut oak - Yellow poplar [Tuliptree] Forest by Shantz and Zon in the "Atlas of American Agriculture, Part I, Section E, Natural Vegetation" in 1924. They described American chestnut, chestnut oak, and tuliptree as being the characteristic species in the primary forest; however "many other kinds of trees [were] found in this forest, in fact, it contain[ed] probably a larger number of species than any other forest area in North America" (p. 196).

Harshberger (1919) described a hillside mixed-deciduous forest community type on a north-facing slope in Delaware County, Pennsylvania, located within the Uplands section of the Piedmont. This community occurred on mica-schist rock with slightly alkaline soils with a deeply stratified leaf litter layer. Harshberger accounted for the slightly alkaline soils through the release of the lime salts during the decay of the leaves of forest trees. He described this forest as dominated by American beech, tuliptree, northern red oak, white oak, black oak, American basswood, and American chestnut, with a subcanopy of American hornbeam and red maple. The shrub stratum dominants included witch hazel, mapleleaf viburnum, northern spicebush, and flowering dogwood. The herbaceous layer was described as "unusually plentiful and diversified" including bloodroot, liverleaf, spring beauty, wild ginger, crane's bill, sweet cicely, rue anemone, jack-in-the-pulpit, miterwort, false Solomon's seal, meadow-rue, Solomon's seal, spleenwort, rattlesnake fern, Christmas fern, and others. Harshberger (1904) identified the same community occurring along Crumb Creek on the campus of Swarthmore College and within Fairmount Park in Philadelphia and claimed these primeval remnants "show[ed] the character of the original forest," which he believed "was a mesophytic one."

Keever (1973) defined three widespread forest types, oak-hickory, chestnut-oak, and a mesophytic community, in the Upland portion of the Piedmont. She indicated that both American beech and sugar maple were more likely to be found on limestone derived soils.

Hickories were found on gentle slopes and flat areas. Chestnut oak was prominent on steeper slopes and quartz bedrock. Northern red oak was more abundant in mesophytic stands with American beech. White oak was found in all stands, but more often on flat areas and gentle slopes. In three secondary stands on limestone soils, she observed many large white oaks and hickories, but observed little to no reproduction of these species.

Gordon (1941) also referenced Darlington's 1826 description of a mesophytic or "rich woods" community occurring within ravines and along watercourses. Tuliptree, white oak, northern red oak, American beech, American chestnut, pignut hickory, and shagbark hickory shared dominance in the canopy, while red maple, white ash, black cherry (*Prunus serotina*), American hornbeam, and flowering dogwood were common subcanopy species. Also present were black walnut and red elm. He noted that American beech expressed dominance on north slopes, while oaks and hickories dominated on south-facing slopes. These "rich woods" most likely occurred on the more mesic Stockton and Ledger Formation soils, like those that occur in Valley Forge NHP north and south of the Schuylkill River (Figure 2). Darlington indicated from his experience that sugar maple was rare in these woods and that it was unlikely that a beech-maple forest occurred in the region and that some phase of "a mixed mesophytic forest was the climactic climax [forest] of the region (p.198) " (Gordon 1941).

Role of American Chestnut in Valley Forge National Historical Park Forests

It is likely that the Dry Oak Forest and the forest community that preceded the Successional Tuliptree Forest at Valley Forge NHP both supported American chestnut prior to the decimation of this species at the turn of the twentieth century. Historical documents were consulted to aid in estimating the appropriate ranges of basal area or percent cover of American chestnut in these forests prior to encampment. American chestnut formerly ranged throughout the east, from Maine southwest through Tennessee, and into the northeast corner of Mississippi. Paleoecological studies indicate that American chestnut migrated to southeastern Pennsylvania from its glacial refuge approximately 2000 years ago. Since the 1900s, there has been an almost complete absence of American chestnut pollen in the record due to the American chestnut blight. Most likely, American chestnut was less abundant than oak in the forests from 1600–1900, as it is slightly less tolerant of fires than are oaks, and has thinner bark and shallower roots than do oaks, but were more tolerant of fires than maples and American beech (Paillet 2002; Foster et al. 2002).

Witness tree data confirm that American chestnut occurred in Valley Forge NHP in the 1700s (Rhoads et al. 1989). American chestnut was mentioned in 5% of the citations and was cited less frequently than hickories and oaks (Rhoads et al. 1989). In the Hopewell Furnace NHS witness tree data 15% of reported trees were American chestnut (Mikan et al. 1994). Oaks and hickories may have been preferred species for recording because they were the biggest trees; however, it is also possible that American chestnut may not have been as abundant in the area at the time.

In a letter describing the Valley Forge encampment prior to tree removal, in 1777, the forest we interpret to be the Dry Oak Forest was described as "rarely interspersed with scrubby American chestnut and hickory" and in the areas where oaks were felled, "hickory, and American chestnut [grew] in abundance and in great perfection" (Wayne 1814). These comments suggest that hickory and American chestnut may both have been less prominent in the forest canopy than oaks were, but were present in the understory. Sprouts were released following the removal of overstory oaks, and eventually these sprouts came to dominate cutover areas.

Braun (1950) describes the abundance of American chestnut at the turn of the twentieth century as occurring throughout the Piedmont subsection of the Oak - Chestnut Region; hence, the historic name of the region. Likewise, American chestnut was reported to comprise up to 50% of the timber by volume on well-drained slopes on non-calcareous substrates in New England and the Appalachians in the early 1900s (Paillet 2002).

In 1904, American chestnut was reported as a prominent component of forests on xeric ridgetops in Chester County, comprising up to 50% of the canopy (Nerurkar 1974). Shreve (1910) indicated that American chestnut was the most abundant tree on the Lower Midland District of the Piedmont Upland in Maryland, with 35% of the trees being American chestnut, 30% black and white oak, and 28% hickories. Whether American chestnut occupied this much of the canopy in pre- and post-encampment forests at Valley Forge NHP is uncertain; however, it was certainly an important component of the wide ranging oak - chestnut forests that dominated the northeastern region from European settlement times (1680) through the encampment period (1777–78), and until the chestnut blight arrived in 1904, as evidenced in pollen analyses, witness tree data, and historical accounts (Rhoads et al. 1989; Mikan et al. 1994; Foster et al. 2002). American chestnut was also most likely a component in the mesophytic forests during this time frame (1680–1904); albeit at lower abundances. In the absence of American chestnut, oaks appear to have increased on drier slopes and ridges, while on more mesic sites, tuliptree has increased (Keever 1973; Overlease 1978).

These accounts suggest that American chestnut was certainly a component of the forests around Valley Forge NHP prior to and at the time of encampment. In the Dry Oak Forest, it was most likely a canopy associate, second to oaks in abundance (Braun 1950). American chestnut sprouts and coarse woody debris were reported in the vegetation mapping plots and in the fenced plots of the Dry-Oak Forest community on Mount Misery at Valley Forge (Heister et al. 2002; Podniesinski et al. 2005). In the Dry – Mesic Chestnut Oak Forest at Valley Forge NHP, where oaks, hickory, American beech, red maple, and tuliptree may have comprised the canopy, American chestnut was most likely present in the canopy, but not a dominant (Harshberger 1919; Gordon 1941; Braun 1950).

Existing Valley Forge National Historical Park Forest Conditions

Vegetation Classification 2005

Mapping of National Vegetation Classification associations at Valley Forge identified two forest communities at Valley Forge NHP: the Dry Oak Forest (*Quercus prinus - Quercus* [*rubra, velutina*] / *Vaccinium angustifolium* Forest) and the Tuliptree – Oak Forest (*Liriodendron tulipifera - Quercus* spp. Forest). Local descriptions for these communities are from Podniesinski et al 2005.

Dry Oak Forest

SYNONYMS:

NVC English Name: Rock Chestnut oak - (Northern Red Oak, Black Oak) / Northern Lowbush Blueberry Forest

NVC Scientific Name: *Quercus prinus - Quercus (rubra, velutina) / Vaccinium angustifolium* Forest

NVC Identifier: CEGL006282

LOCAL DESCRIPTION

Environmental Description: This community occurs on well-drained soils on moderate to steep slopes; primarily on Mount Joy and Mount Misery.

Vegetation Description: This type is most common on the slopes of Mount Joy and Mount Misery within the park. The canopy is dominated by drought-tolerant chestnut oak (*Quercus prinus*) and black oak (*Quercus velutina*), with blackgum (*Nyssa sylvatica*) and scarlet oak (*Quercus coccinea*) as occasional codominants. The subcanopy is characterized by moderate to dense cover of blackgum, red maple (*Acer rubrum*), and sassafras (*Sassafras albidum*). The tall-shrub layer is often diagnostic for this type, characterized by moderate to dense cover of mountain laurel (*Kalmia latifolia*). In some stands, the tall-shrub layer is dominated by young blackgum. Also common in the tall-shrub layer are red maple (*Acer rubrum*), sassafras (*Sassafras albidum*), and witch-hazel (*Hamamelis virginiana*). The low-shrub and herbaceous layers are typically very sparse or absent, presumably due to heavy deer browsing. The low-shrub layer, when present, is limited to seedlings of canopy trees and a few ericad species: lowbush blueberry (*Vaccinium pallidum*), black huckleberry (*Gaylussacia baccata*), and pink azalea (*Rhododendron periclymenoides*). Herbaceous plants typically occur as solitary individuals or small clumps, when present. Common herbaceous species include pipsissewa (*Chimaphila maculata*), hay-scented fern (*Dennstaedtia punctilobula*), marginal woodfern (*Dryopteris marginalis*), and Indian cucumber-root.

On more moderate slopes and areas with more mesic soils, this community is more variable. Canopy dominants are still dry-site oaks (chestnut oak, black oak and scarlet oak) but may also include a greater proportion of other hardwood species, including white oak (*Quercus alba*), red maple, tuliptree (*Liriodendron tulipifera*), American beech (*Fagus grandifolia*), and sassafras (*Sassafras albidum*). A subcanopy is usually present, characterized by a mix of hardwood species such as red maple, sassafras, American beech, chestnut oak and black oak. Typical tall shrubs include flowering dogwood (*Cornus florida*), witch-hazel and mountain laurel. The tall-shrub layer varies from sparse to abundant, with flowering dogwood exceeding 50% cover in some locations. The low-shrub and herbaceous layers are very sparse to nearly absent, presumably the result of intense deer browsing. The low-shrub layer is characterized by seedlings of the canopy and subcanopy woody species. Typical herb species include garlic mustard (*Alliaria petiolata*), Japanese stiltgrass (*Microstegium vimineum*), and Pennsylvania sedge (*Carex pensylvanica*).

Most Abundant Species:

Stratum	Lifeform	Species
Tree canopy	Broad-leaved deciduous tree	chestnut oak, black oak
Tree subcanopy	Broad-leaved deciduous tree	blackgum

Characteristic Species: mountain laurel, black oak, chestnut oak

Other Comments:[5] Of the three natural upland forest types in the park, this Dry Oak Forest is the most mature and least disturbed with respect to invasive species. It was also one of the more difficult vegetation types to characterize as it graded from very dry oak forest at the top of Mount Misery to dry-mesic forest along the toe slope with Valley Creek. Attempts to separate the dry from the dry-mesic oak forest was not easily represented in mapping. As a result, only one Dry Oak Forest association was recognized at the time the vegetation map was produced.

The Dry Oak Forest appears to be resistant to many of the invasive species common in the rest of the park, possibly due to drier, less fertile soils. Deer herbivory threatens the long-term persistence of this and other forest types in the park through the browsing of tree seedlings. Deer browsing also appears to be depressing native wildflower populations.

Local Description Authors: J. Lundgren and G. Podniesinski.

---

[5] The "Additional Comments" fields in both descriptions were added subsequently by the authors of this paper.

INTERIOR MID- TO LATE-SUCCESSIONAL TULIPTREE - HARDWOOD UPLAND FOREST (ACID TYPE)

SYNONYMS:

NVC English Name:	**Tuliptree - Oak species Forest**
NVC Scientific Name:	***Liriodendron tulipifera - Quercus* spp. Forest**
NVC Identifier:	**CEGL007221**

LOCAL DESCRIPTION

Environmental Description: This community occurs in areas that were cleared or created by fill, usually on mesic soils. Some of the stands at Valley Forge National Historical Park were planted. Tuliptree seeds-in abundantly on cleared land and is a characteristic early-successional tree of this region.

Vegetation Description: This type is found throughout Valley Forge National Historical Park as mid-successional and mature forest stands. Some of these stands appear to have been planted 70 to 80 years ago. The most characteristic feature of this type is the dominance of tuliptree (*Liriodendron tulipifera*). Tuliptree is the only dominant in many stands, with black oak (*Quercus velutina*) and white ash (*Fraxinus americana*) codominant or subdominant in others. Other occasional canopy trees include red maple (*Acer rubrum*), northern red oak (*Quercus rubra*), and sassafras (*Sassafras albidum*). The subcanopy is usually open (typically less than 30% total cover, though may approach 50%), characterized by tuliptree, red maple, tall individuals of flowering dogwood (*Cornus florida*), blackgum (*Nyssa sylvatica*), occasional redbud (*Cercis canadensis*), and sassafras. The shrub layer is also open and appears to be pruned below 1.5 m by heavy deer browsing. Typical shrub species are flowering dogwood (clear dominant in the shrub layer), spicebush (*Lindera benzoin*), black haw (*Viburnum prunifolium*), mountain laurel (*Kalmia latifolia*), and the nonnative *Lonicera japonica*. The herbaceous layer has very low diversity and is dominated by exotics. The herbaceous layer is typically a dense growth of Japanese stiltgrass (*Microstegium vimineum*), except in stands with a very dense canopy, in which case there may be a high proportion of bare ground. Other common species, besides Japanese stiltgrass, include garlic mustard (*Alliaria petiolata*), low smartweed (*Polygonum caespitosum*), jack-in-the-pulpit (*Arisaema triphyllum*), and clearweed (*Pilea pumila*). Indicator species that occur here, but typically not in the oak forests, include downy Solomon's-seal (*Polygonatum pubescens*), black snakeroot (*Sanicula marilandica*), and small enchanter's nightshade (*Circaea alpina*).

Liriodendron tulipifera is particularly abundant in this type but can be an important component of many forest types in the region. At Valley Forge, downy Solomon's-seal (*Polygonatum pubescens*), black snakeroot (*Sanicula marilandica*), and small enchanter's nightshade (*Circaea alpina*) are differential species in the herb layer.

Most Abundant Species:

Stratum	Lifeform	Species
Tree canopy	Broad-leaved deciduous tree	*Liriodendron tulipifera*
Tree subcanopy	Broad-leaved deciduous tree	*Acer rubrum*, *Liriodendron tulipifera*
Tall shrub/sapling	Broad-leaved deciduous shrub	*Cornus florida*
Herb (field)	Graminoid	*Microstegium vimineum*

Characteristic Species: *Circaea alpina, Liriodendron tulipifera, Polygonatum pubescens, Sanicula marilandica*

Other Comments: The tuliptree – oak forest is a disturbed forest type, typically with abundant invasive species, especially Japanese stiltgrass (*Microstegium vimineum*). As with the Dry Oak Forest, little or no forest regeneration is occurring and all woody plants within reach of deer are heavily browsed.

Local Description Authors: J. Lundgren and G. Podniesinski

<u>Understory Data from Valley Forge National Historical Park Deer Exclosures</u>

An inventory of the herb, shrub, and seedling composition within both forest types was conducted in fenced and unfenced plots at the park in 1993, 1995, and 1998 (Heister et al 2002). The tree seedling and sapling data from the fenced plots provide some insight to the potential composition of the future forest in the absence of deer browse; however, these data should be interpreted with some caution, because the complete absence of deer browse is a similarly unnatural state. The unfenced plots were too heavily impacted by deer browse to provide insight into past and future forest types.

Herb diversity in Dry Oak Forests is naturally low compared to that of mesophytic forests in general. This is reflected in the fenced plots where the diversity of the native herbaceous flora of the Successional Tuliptree community is greater than that of the Dry Oak Forests, despite also being more heavily invaded by exotic plants. While of low cover, the presence of some of the native species is noteworthy. Many of the native herbs identified in the fenced plots are slow-colonizing species that are cited as occurring more frequently in ancient forests of the United States (Verheyen et al. 2003). Examples of these slow colonizing, mesic forest herbs found in the Successional Tuliptree Forest exclosures included wild ginger, Carolina crane's-bill (*Geranium carolinianum*), liverleaf, Indian cucumber root, American ginseng (*Panax quinquefolius*), may-apple, smooth Solomon's seal, sweet cicely, bloodroot, trillium (*Trillium* spp.), and bellwort (*Uvularia perfoliata*). Some of these species may have persisted in localized forest patches within the former agricultural landscape (Bellemare 2002). Additional fenced plot mesic forest herbs more typical of successional forests include jack-in-the pulpit, white wood aster, wild boneset (*Eupatorium rugosum*), licorice bedstraw (*Galium circaezans*), sweet-scented bedstraw (*Galium triflorum*), rattlesnake root, hairy Solomon's seal, false Solomon's seal, heartleaf foamflower (*Tiarella cordifolia*), and sessile-leaf bellwort (Verheyen et al. 2003).

Many mesic species cited above are also referenced in Harshberger's (1919) "unusually plentiful and diversified" herbaceous layer described in mesophytic forests he encountered in southeastern Pennsylvania. A 1901 bird census in Berwyn, Chester County, describes a secondary forest dominated by oaks, hickories, tulip poplar, American beech, and red maple, and also lists some of the same herbaceous species (Unknown 1901). Likewise, Braun (1950) refers to a diverse herbaceous layer associated with the mesophytic forest in the Piedmont Upland of southeastern Pennsylvania.

Ecological Stressors in the Valley Forge National Historical Park Forests

Recent anthropogenic factors influence the existing vegetation patterns and species composition of the Valley Forge NHP forests that were not prevalent in these forests at the time of encampment. Tree regeneration in all forest communities is threatened by an increasing abundance of white-tailed deer which browse the understory and consume tree seedlings, saplings, and herbaceous plants. Carfioli (2006) reported that the white-tailed deer population within Valley Forge NHP between 1997 and 2006 increased from 400 deer/km^2 (154 deer/mi^2) (772 individuals) to 632 deer/km^2 (244 deer/mi^2) (1,218 individuals). Historical deer populations at the time of European settlement in the early 1700s ranged between 18–31 deer/km^2 (7–12 deer/mi^2) (McCabe and McCabe 1997). Heister et al. (2002) noted that the density recommended by the Pennsylvania Game Commission for wooded areas of Chester and

Montgomery counties as 8–12 deer/km^2 (3–5 deer/mi^2), and that deCalesta (1997) reported that tree seedling species richness, abundance, and tree sapling height significantly declined in the Allegheny National Forest in Pennsylvania at a deer density of 7.7 deer/ km^2 (3 deer/mi^2).

Aggressive invasive exotic plants present at Valley Forge NHP have the potential to outcompete native plants for limited resources. Heister et al. (2002) reported that herbaceous and vine plant communities on Mount Joy were dominated by nonnative species, and that "nonnative species were unaffected by deer browse and thus will likely continue to increase in dominance within woodlands at Valley Forge NHP" (p. 20).

The nonnative gypsy moth is another stressor to Valley Forge NHP forests. A gypsy moth infestation during the 1980s and through 1992 resulted in canopy mortality of oak trees at the park (Cypher et al. 1985). Although as of this writing no oak defoliation by gypsy moths has occurred at the park since 1992, future gypsy moth outbreaks are a potential threat (Carfioli 2006b). A heavy decline in oak dominance could potentially alter the composition in favor of successional hardwoods such as red maple, and perhaps alter the successional pathway over the long term (Overlease 1987).

Fire suppression over the last 60 years has favored thin-barked, shade-tolerant species in the understory over oak regeneration in eastern old-growth oak and oak-hickory forests (White and White 1996). Foster et al. (2002) note that periodic fires are required to maintain New England forests characterized by oak and chestnut. For oaks to regenerate, an opening in the canopy greater than 150 m^2 (1,615 ft^2) is required, while advanced regeneration of more shade-tolerant species requires only a single tree-sized canopy gap (Frelich and Reich 1996).

Adjacent land use also plays a role in forest condition. Stand surface area with considerable edge limits dispersal distances for native plant regeneration, limits home range size for animals, and increases the susceptibility of the stand to higher intensity disturbances. Forest stands at Valley Forge NHP are relatively small in area, resulting in a high ratio of edge to interior. The majority of the Successional Tuliptree Forests are located adjacent to fields and roads (Figure 1).

Potential Trajectory of Valley Forge National Historical Park Forests Assuming No Management Actions

NPS Management Policies (2001) state "the [National Park] Service recognizes that natural processes and species are evolving, and will allow this evolution to continue, minimally influenced by human actions" and that "the term 'natural condition' is used here to describe the condition that would occur in the absence of human dominance over the landscape ... ." These policies recommend minimal interference with natural communities except "to restore natural ecosystem functioning that has been disrupted by past or ongoing human activities." The Dry Oak community at Valley Forge NHP may not require intensive management over time because it has a greater proportion of native species and a history of less disturbance than does the Successional Tuliptree Forest; however, the Successional Tuliptree Forest is itself an unnatural community that has come to dominate the Valley Forge NHP landscape as a result of past human activities.

Seedling and sapling data cited in the Bowersox and Larrick (1999) and the Heister et al. (2002) reports were reviewed to provide some insight into future forest composition. Although there are some limitations to predicting forest composition from these sources, they are the only reports containing data about seedlings and saplings protected from deer browse at Valley Forge NHP. Vegetation composition within the fenced plots is not a completely realistic representation of projected composition because some deer browse is a natural component of the ecosystem. However, the presence of species inside the fenced plots are likely to have persisted in the seed bank or were transported from similar vegetation stands nearby and are good indicators of the potential community. The limitation of the Bowersox and Larrick (1999) study is that the data provided for Valley Forge NHP cover the entire park and is not specific to either the Dry Oak or the Successional Tuliptree communities. Investigation of soil seed banks would provide additional information to complement the data from deer exclosure plots.

In the Successional Tuliptree Forest community, black cherry, red maple, white ash, and blackgum were the most abundant tree seedlings and saplings in the fenced plots. Northern red oak seedlings and saplings were present, but of lower density. Chestnut oak and white oak seedlings were also present, but fewer in number than the northern red oak seedlings. Occasional hickory, American beech, and Norway maple (*Acer platanoides*) seedlings were also observed in these plots. The statistically significant tree regeneration indicators for the tuliptree forest were eastern redbud and white ash (Gawler 2002). The presence of oak, American beech, and hickory seedlings in exclosure plots suggests that these species also occurred in the forest canopy. In the unfenced plots, there were virtually no tree seedlings or saplings under 1.8 m (6 ft) (Heister et al. 2002).

In Dry Oak Forest deer exclosure plots, northern red oak seedlings were the most abundant, followed by chestnut oak, sassafras, black cherry, red maple, and blackgum. Red maple, chestnut oak, and sassafras were the tree regeneration indicators for the Dry Oak community (Gawler 2002). Podniesinski et al. (2005) described the tall-shrub layer of the Dry Oak community as dominated by young blackgum saplings, with red maple and sassafras both common. Bowersox and Larrick (1999) reported that maple and blackgum also were the dominant sapling-sized trees on Mount Misery and Mount Joy, where most of the Dry Oak community occurs in Valley Forge NHP (Figure 1). American beech and tuliptree seedlings also occurred occasionally in the fenced plots within this community. American beech has been cited as a suppressed understory species in some Oak-Chestnut stands in the Upland portion of the Piedmont (Keever 1973). Only one white oak seedling was observed within the fenced plots in each of this and the Dry Oak Forest type. In the unfenced plots, there was no oak reproduction (Gawler 2002; Heister et al. 2002).

Abrams (2003) indicates a decline in white oak throughout the east coast since pre-European settlement times (early 1600s) and reports that red maple, chestnut oak, and northern red oak have increased in its place in present-day forests as a result of repeated cutting of oak forests, high-grading of white oaks, and fire suppression. Even with protection from deer browse, oak regeneration in the Valley Forge NHP forests is low, as is typical for present-day oak forests in much of the northeast (Heister et al. 2002; Podniesinski et al. 2005). The Dry Oak community may maintain itself over time (+/-100 years) if the appropriate stressors and/or impacts of those stressors are managed at the stand level to provide an opportunity for the oak regeneration to survive and mature.

In the absence of stand-maintaining disturbances, such as fire, cutting, or a form of stand management that mimics a disturbance, the Dry Oak Forests existing today may no longer exist in future centuries. Without oak regeneration they may be replaced by red maple-dominated forests. In the Successional Tuliptree community any remaining oaks will most likely be outcompeted by other shade-tolerant species in the understory and the forest will maintain itself as a tuliptree-dominated community.

The occurrence of exotic vine species such as Oriental bittersweet (*Celastrus orbiculatus*) and Japanese honeysuckle in the Successional Tuliptree forest type may influence future forest dynamics and composition (Davis et al. 2004). These species can effectively smother other vegetation, preventing their growth and thereby inhibiting succession. Japanese stilt grass is also an aggressive shade-tolerant exotic grass that can overtake entire forest understories. These exotic plants have the potential to shade out native herbs, tree seedlings, and shrubs in the understory once they are established. White-tailed deer do browse some exotic species at Valley Forge NHP and may effectively control infestations of some exotic plants (Heister et al. 2006); however, deer generally avoid Japanese stilt grass (Southeast Exotic Pest Plan Council 2005).

The future trajectory of the Successional Tuliptree Forest without active management is most likely towards a homogeneous hardwood forest dominated by tuliptree, red maple, white ash, black cherry, and blackgum. With understory tree seedlings and saplings browsed and limited survival of tree regeneration this community will persist as a tuliptree-dominated community. The Dry Oak community may also experience a shift in canopy composition without active management, as there is no oak regeneration in the seedling and sapling layers outside of the exclosures. With red maple, sassafras, and blackgum present in the subcanopy, shrub, and seedling layers of this community, those species may be favored, particularly under current browse levels.

Desired Conditions

A target vegetation type on the sites currently occupied by the Dry Oak Forest is a high-quality example of the same vegetation type that currently exists (Figure 1 and Figure 6). The desired condition is an old growth stand of essentially the same composition and structure, but lacking exotic species and supporting tree regeneration. A notable absence from the current canopy composition is American chestnut, an abundant component of the target Dry Oak Forest. Relatively large examples of Dry Oak Forest at Valley Forge NHP may support reintroduced American chestnut with a target composition of 25–50% canopy cover. More specific descriptions of the environmental conditions, vegetation structure and composition, stand dynamics, old-growth reference sites, and old-growth stand metrics for a target Dry Oak community are discussed below. Down slope of the Dry Oak Forest occurs a forest described by Podniesinski et al. (2005) as a mesic variant of the Dry Oak Forest. Further investigation following the completion of Podniesinski et al.'s work suggests that that variant may be more appropriately classified as a separate NVC type, the Dry-Mesic Chestnut Oak Forest (*Quercus prinus – Quercus rubra / Hamamelis virginiana* Forest). Determination of whether the currently described variant may be classified as a separate NVC type can be made only with examination of individual plot data, which is beyond the scope of this project. Regardless of the classification of the existing vegetation, the desired forest type on the soils derived from the Cambrian

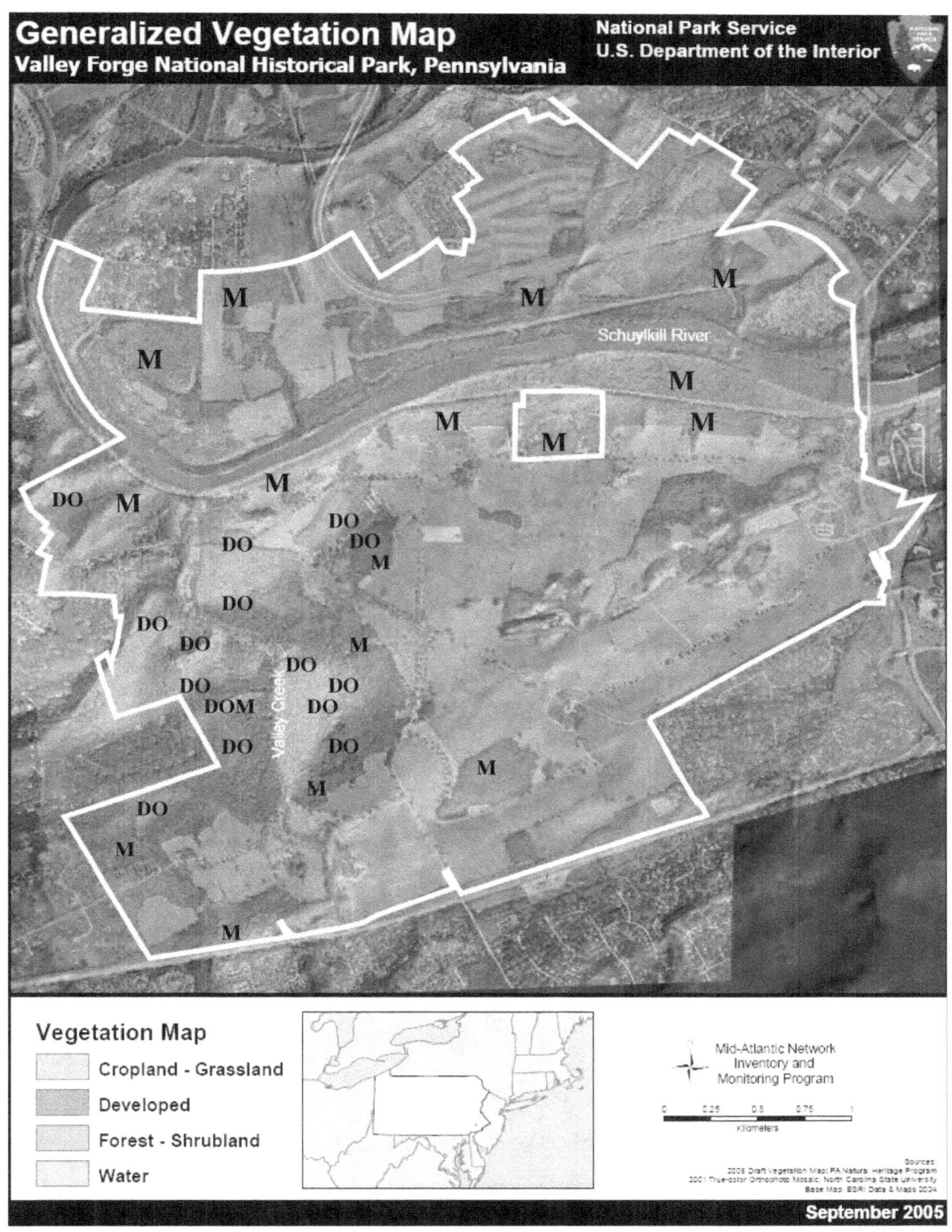

Figure 6. Proposed potential locations for target forest types of Dry Oak (DO) Forest, Dry-Mesic Chestnut Oak (DOM) Forest, and Mesophytic (M) Forest at Valley Forge National Historical Park (Image adapted from Davis et al. 2006)

Antietam and Harpers Formation is a high-quality example of the Dry-Mesic Chestnut Oak Forest (Figure 6).

A target vegetation type on the Valley Forge NHP sites currently occupied by the Successional Tuliptree Forest community, particularly the limestone / dolostone soils and sandstone, mudstone, and siltstone soils associated with the Triassic Stockton and Cambrian Ledger Formations, is a Mesophytic forest community. Site conditions associated with this community are gradual lower slopes and flat terrain and steeper north facing slopes that serve as natural fire breaks (Figure 6). The recommended species composition of this community is an admixture of oaks, American beech, tuliptree, hickories, and red maple in the canopy and subcanopy, with a diverse herbaceous layer similar to Darlington's "rich woods" described by Gordon (1941) and Harshberger's "rich woods" descriptions from 1904 and 1919.

Having described the historical and current conditions of two forest types at Valley Forge National Historical Park, we now proceed to defining a vision of the conditions desired for these two forest types if they were to develop without the influence of human-induced stressors. These are described by the "A" level criteria which are represented, in part, by old-growth reference sites. Old-growth stands of these forest types do not fully meet the criteria at the "A" level because they exist as considerably smaller patches than they would under ideal conditions. Small patch sizes increase the potential for exotic species to invade, are subjected to increased herbivory, decrease the amount of habitat for larger animals supported by large, pristine forest patches, and do not support large-scale disturbance regimes. However, old growth sites provide us with important information on stand structure, soil structure, composition of woody debris, and species composition. The "A" level criteria, as well as the B," "C," and "D" criteria (still to be developed) allow managers to evaluate current conditions in relation to desired conditions.

DRY OAK FOREST "A" LEVEL CRITERIA[6]

Valley Forge Name:	**Dry Oak Forest**
NVC Name:	***Quercus prinus - Quercus (rubra, velutina) / Vaccinium angustifolium* Forest**
NVC Code:	**CEGL006282**

Target Environmental Condition: This forest occurs on dry, shallow, acidic, infertile, well-drained soils on a variety of geological formations forming ridges and steep slopes that are often south-facing. It can also occur on slightly more permeable soils on more level topography. Often these forests occur on south and west facing slopes, but can also occur across entire ridgetops. The geological formations include gneisses, schist, conglomerate, quartz, monzonite, Triassic sandstone, and quartzite. A well developed leaf litter layer that burns easily occurs in this community, although it may be thinner on steeper slopes. Soil decomposition rates are low.

Target Vegetation Structure and Composition: The canopy dominants include chestnut oak, black oak, and American chestnut with less frequent white oak, scarlet oak, and northern red oak. Scattered tuliptree may also be present in the canopy. Red maple, blackgum, and flowering dogwood are typical subcanopy trees. The low-shrub layer is well-developed and comprised chiefly of ericaceous species, including early lowbush blueberry, black huckleberry, and / or wintergreen (*Gualtheria procumbens*). A tall-shrub layer is generally lacking but, when present, may include mountain laurel, mapleleaf viburnum, witch hazel, and pink azalea. The herbaceous layer is inconspicuous. Striped pipsissewa may be present. Pink lady's slipper (*Cypripedium acaule*) may be present, but is not common. Seedlings and saplings from the canopy are also common. The canopy is relatively open, allowing for oak regeneration in the understory. The largest canopy trees have diameters at breast height up to and on occasion exceeding 90 cm (3 feet) and are represented by multiple age classes within the stand. Additional quantitative stand metrics are described in the next section.

Target Species Composition:

Stratum	Lifeform	Species	Target Canopy Cover
Tree canopy	Broad-leaved deciduous tree	chestnut oak	20–40%
Tree canopy	Broad-leaved deciduous tree	black oak	10–40%
Tree canopy	Broad-leaved deciduous tree	American chestnut	25–50%
Tree canopy	Broad-leaved deciduous tree	scarlet oak	5–15%
Tree canopy	Broad-leaved deciduous tree	white oak	2–10%
Tree canopy	Broad-leaved deciduous tree	northern red oak	2–10%
Tree canopy	Broad-leaved deciduous tree	tuliptree	3–5%
Tree subcanopy	Broad-leaved deciduous tree	red maple	10–25%
Tree subcanopy	Broad-leaved deciduous tree	blackgum	10–20%
Tree subcanopy	Broad-leaved deciduous tree	flowering dogwood	5–20%

---

[6] As previously noted, we describe the highest quality or "A" level criteria for target forest types. Criteria describing stands of lower but acceptable quality can be derived, but are beyond the scope of the current project.

Stratum	Lifeform	Species	Target Canopy Cover
Tall shrub	Broad-leaved evergreen shrub	mountain laurel	2–15%
Tall shrub	Broad-leaved deciduous shrub	mapleleaf viburnum	2–10%
Tall shrub	Broad-leaved deciduous shrub	witch hazel	1–3%
Tall shrub	Broad-leaved evergreen shrub	pink azalea	1–3%
Low shrub	Broad-leaved deciduous shrub	early lowbush blueberry	50–75%
Low shrub	Broad-leaved deciduous shrub	black huckleberry	35–60%
Low shrub	Broad-leaved evergreen shrub	wintergreen	5–20%

Target Dynamics: Windthrow, lightning, fire and ice damage are common natural disturbances in this community. Low-intensity periodic ground fires set every 5–40 years and infrequent canopy fires every 100–500 years maintain oak regeneration and community stability over time (Frelich and Reich 1996; Abrams 1992, Nowacki 1993). This disturbance regime reduces understory competition for oak regeneration (Nowacki 1993; White and White, 1996). Flowering dogwood, mapleleaf viburnum and blueberries are also adapted to periodic fires. Forests on these more xeric sites will most likely maintain stability since few replacement species can tolerate the conditions (Nowacki 1993).

Old Growth Reference Sites: Reference sites were researched for this forest community in the same ecoregional and geographic area with similar site conditions.

- One example of an old growth chestnut oak stand was identified near the Hopewell Furnace National Historic Site and was studied and described by Mikan et al. in 1994. This community is dominated by old growth chestnut oak, black birch (*Betula lenta*), red maple, yellow birch (*Betula allegheniensis*), blackgum, northern red oak and black oak. This study also described the surrounding forest using witness tree data that was very similar in species composition to the Valley Forge NHP witness tree data.

- Abrams (2003) describes a mature forest that we interpret to be the Dry Oak community at Coleman Hollow on Savage Mountain in western Maryland with a canopy dominated by red maple (24%), chestnut oak (23%), white oak (20%), northern red oak (14%), and black oak (9%). He also describes an example of this community at South Savage, also on Savage Mountain, dominated by chestnut oak (20%), black birch (18%), northern red oak (17%), red maple (17%), black oak (11%), and white oak (6%).

References: Gordon 1941, Overlease 1978, Braun 1950, Harshberger 1919, Nowacki 1993, Gaines et al. 1997; Abrams 2003; Mikan et al. 1994

Target Ecological Integrity Metrics for Dry Oak Forest "A" Level Criteria[7]

A summary of Dry Oak Forest target values or ranges compared to existing conditions at Valley Forge NHP for the following ecological integrity metrics is provided in Table 3 at the end of this criteria section.

Stand metrics:

Stand Structural Class: Based on stand density estimates of McCarthy et al. (2003), Mikan et al. (1994), and others, we recommend a possible target stand basal area of 25–30 m^2/ha (100–130 ft^2/ac) and a possible target stand density of 350 ($\geq$10 cm) trees/ha (141 trees/ac). According to Abrams and others (1995), old-growth chestnut oak and white oak forests exhibit continuous tree recruitment under the oak-dominated canopy over time, leading to an uneven aged structure. This recruitment results in >1,000 oak seedlings/ha (>405 oak seedlings/ac), and considerably less oak saplings—approximately 10–100/ha (25–40/ac) in the understory (Mikan et al. 1994; Abrams et al. 1995). Possible target tree seedling and sapling densities for this community are 5,400 seedlings/ha (2186 seedlings / ac) and 500 saplings/ha (202 saplings/ac) (Mikan et al. 1994).

A target distribution of structural classes for a high quality Dry Oak community consists of tree species from the canopy in every size and age class, maintained over time. Oaks will dominate the largest diameter size classes, while red maple, blackgum, and sassafras will dominate the smaller size classes. Natural disturbance regimes of windthrow and lightning fires in combination with periodic surface fires maintain the multi-aged structural class distribution of this community, allowing for regeneration in the understory. Under these disturbance regimes the understory will be more open than without disturbance.

Canopy Closure: Canopy closure of 70–80% is recommended for high quality examples of this community. To maintain this condition, the canopy should be partially opened every 100–200 years by intense canopy disturbances such as partial canopy fire or partial overstory cut (Frelich and Reich 1996). Minor disturbances (surface fires, wind, and harvest) every 21 years will also maintain oak regeneration. Sustaining these disturbances prevents invasion and replacement by shade-tolerant species (Frelich and Reich 1996).

Snag Abundance: A target average snag abundance for this community at Valley Forge NHP is 25 standing snags/ha (10 standing snags/ac) $\geq$10 cm (4 in) dbh (Johnson and Schnell [1985] cited in Gaines et al. 1997). Snag abundance is variable in old-growth Dry Oak Forests, as it is dependent on disturbances, including disease, insects, and wind, rather than single-tree mortality. Snag abundance is greater in these forests after a canopy or partial-canopy killing disturbance. Intense canopy fires set every 100–400 years will increase snag abundance periodically.

Coarse Woody Debris (CWD): An estimated possible target for CWD for this community is 25–50 tons/ha (10–20 tons/ac) with dbh >10 cm (4 in) (Whitbeck 1995; Gaines et al. 1997). CWD biomass is also variable in old-growth Dry Oak Forests, as it, like snag abundance, is dependent on disturbances, including disease, insects, and wind, rather than just single-tree

---

[7] The following metrics refer to the Dry Oak Community. While the metrics are likely to be similar to those of the Dry-Mesic Oak Forest, the development of those metrics was beyond the scope of this report.

mortality. As a result, CWD is patchily distributed in space as it is episodically produced (White and White 1996). In the absence of an intense disturbance, canopy mortality from old age, lightning, and windthrow will contribute minor amounts of CWD to the forest floor; thereby, maintaining a relatively stable amount of CWD accumulation until the next disturbance event.

Photopoints: Potential representative vegetation plots of this community (in its young stage) from the Valley Forge NHP vegetation mapping project include VAFO.20, VAFO.21, VAFO.23, and VAFO.24 (Podniesinski et al. 2005).

Tree Metrics:

Tree Condition: A desired condition of trees in this community at Valley Forge NHP is that of robust, large diameter, spreading-crowned trees. Estimates of diameter size for the largest canopy species include black oak: 91 cm (3 ft); chestnut oak: 91 cm (3 ft); American chestnut: 61 cm (2 ft); and sassafras: 76 cm (2.5 ft) (Harshberger 1904; Mikan et al. 1994; Gaines et al. 1997). All tree species are represented in smaller diameter classes as well. The large diameter oaks have no heavy lower branches or branch scars and boles without branches to the crown; long distances to their first branches in the crown, and flat-topped or spreading crowns (White and White 1996). The condition of American chestnut declined in this community over time and a desired condition is to restore American chestnut coverage in these stands to between 25–50% of the canopy. Oak condition may decline in response to gypsy moth outbreaks.

Tree growth and mortality rates: A target age for trees in a desired Valley Forge NHP Dry Oak Forest is at least 150 years old, and at least 50% the majority of the dominant canopy trees have reached life expectancy and/or are older than average interval between large-scale disturbances. (Frelich and Reich 1996). Large-scale disturbances in these forests occur between 100–400 years. The target net annual growth of this forest type is zero (White and White 1996).

Tree regeneration: This community supports oak and American chestnut regeneration in all size and age classes over at least 100 years until the next canopy disturbance. Possible target tree seedling and sapling densities for this community are 5,400 seedlings/ha (2186 seedlings/ac) and 500 saplings/ha (202 saplings/ac) (Mikan et al. 1994). A target seedling density for oak species in this community is approximately 1,300–5,000 oak seedlings/ha (526–2,024 seedlings/ac) and from 10–100 oak saplings/ha (4–40 saplings/ac). While oaks produce many seedlings, very few grow into the sapling stage (Abrams et al. 1995). The majority of the saplings in this community are American chestnut sprouts, red maple, and blackgum. The canopy must be opened by a disturbance such as a canopy fire every 100 years and small scale understory fires must occur every 20 years; and deer browse must be significantly reduced. The amount of regeneration in this Dry Oak Forest is directly linked to these disturbances (White and White 1996).

Understory Metrics:

Indicator Plants: The characteristic plants in this community include chestnut oak, American chestnut, blackgum, flowering dogwood, mountain laurel, mapleleaf viburnum, early lowbush blueberry. The herbaceous stratum is inconspicuous.

Exotic Plants: A desired condition of the Old-growth Dry Oak Forests at Valley Forge is absence of exotic species within the core of the forest stands. High quality examples of this community maintain a low-light condition, have dry acidic soils, and a dense understory dominated by ericaceous shrubs, blueberry, and mountain laurel. These conditions are typically unfavorable to exotics. Fragmented stands with exposed edges, roads, or trails, however, are more likely to be invaded and are lower quality examples of this community.

Understory diversity: A desired understory composition of this community is neither species rich nor diverse. It is comprised of a relatively open shrub layer with scattered mountain laurel, mapleleaf viburnum, and saplings from the canopy. The low-shrub layer is dominated by blueberries. There are virtually no herbaceous species present. These understory species are adapted and maintained by periodic fires every 20 years (Overlease 1987). Provided disturbance regimes are present, the understory diversity will remain stable and not decline over time. Exotic invasive plant species are atypical in the understory. Deer browse is a major stress to understory health and diversity and a limited browse pressure is a recommended desired condition.

Soil metrics:

Forest Floor Composition: Proposed desired conditions of the Valley Forge NHP Dry Oak Forest floor include a well developed leaf litter layer that is conducive to burning. After a fire, the litter will be shallow. Pit and mound microtopography is not characteristic of this community because of the fire regime that maintains this stand, which does not typically uproot trees (White and White 1996).

Soil chemistry: Target soils are deep, with a well developed soil profile. The soil is acidic with an approximate pH range of 4.0–4.5. Decomposition rates are slow. The soils are well drained and typically occur on gneiss, schist, quartz, monzonite, Triassic sandstone, quartzite, and/or conglomerate geological formations.

Landscape Metrics:

Landscape context: The minimal interior patch size should be 8 ha (20 ac), but larger stands (10 ha or more) are recommended to support characteristic fauna, to support dispersal among patches, and to reduce edge effect[8]. The desired shape of the patch is circular and wide, rather than linear, to maintain the core old-growth forest conditions. Stand shape should minimize edge; a recommended ratio of stand area to disturbance patch size is 50:1 to ensure optimal regeneration (White and White 1996).

---

[8] Note that this metric provides a minimum threshold so is not considered "A" level. More data are needed to determine upper thresholds for stand size

Table 3. Summary of target ecological integrity metrics compared to existing forest conditions (where measured or known) for Valley Forge National Historical Park Dry Oak Forests.

Metric	Sub metric	Target Ranges for Old-growth Dry Oak Community	Existing Conditions for Valley Forge NHP Dry Oak Community
Stand structural class	Basal Area	25–30 m2/ha (100–130 ft2/ac)	These metrics need to be determined for existing Dry Oak community. Data from Bowersox and Larrick (1999) is not community specific for direct comparison
	Tree density	average of 350 (>10 cm dbh) trees/ha (140 trees/ac)	
	Age	multiple age classes	
	Structure	multiple structural classes	
Canopy closure		70–80%	70–80%
Snag abundance		average of 25 standing snags/ha (10 standing snags/ac) >10 cm (4 in dbh)	needs to be determined
Coarse woody debris		25–50 tons/ha (10–20 tons/ac) dbh >10 cm (4 in)	needs to be determined
Tree condition	Overall	large diameter, healthy robust trees with spreading crowns	Oak mortality from 1980's gypsy moth epidemic, but good canopy recovery from disturbance; American chestnut no longer in canopy from blight
	DBH estimates	61–91+ cm dbh (2–3+ ft dbh)	Need to analyze Plots data more closely but average Dry Oak diameters were 40 cm dbh (16 in) and ranged from 12–70 cm (5–28 in) dbh
Tree growth and mortality rates	Age	150+ years for canopy trees	80–100 years?
	Net annual growth	zero	Greater than zero
	Mortality rate	50% the majority of the dominant canopy trees have reached life expectancy and/or are older than average interval between large-scale disturbances (every 100–400 years)	Undetermined, but most likely less than 50% of the dominant canopy trees in the Dry Oak community have reached life expectancy
Tree regeneration	Sapling density	500 saplings/ha (202 saplings/ac)	These metrics need to be determined. Data from Bowersox and Larrick (1999) may be related, but not community specific for direct comparison.
	Seedling density	5,400 seedlings/ha (2186 seedlings/ac)	
	Stressors	None	deer browse, exotics, lack of stand regenerating disturbance regime
Indicator plants		chestnut oak, chestnut, black-gum, flowering dogwood, mountain laurel, mapleleaf viburnum, blueberries	chestnut oak, black oak, mountain laurel
Exotic plants		Zero	garlic mustard and Japanese stiltgrass common herbs in mesic Dry Oak community; few exotics in Dry Oak community
Understory diversity	Species richness	low	low
	Dominant species	blueberries, few herbs	blueberries

Table 3. Summary of target ecological integrity metrics compared to existing forest conditions (where measured or known) for Valley Forge National Historical Park Dry Oak Forests (continued).

Metric	Sub metric	Target Ranges for Old-growth Dry Oak Community	Existing Conditions for Valley Forge NHP Dry Oak Community
Forest floor condition	Leaf litter layer	thick, well developed	thick, well developed
	Microtopography	pit and mound uncharacteristic	pit and mound uncharacteristic
Soil chemistry	Soil history-landuse	forested; not converted to agriculture	forested; not converted to agriculture; cleared for fuelwood
	Soil profile	well developed and undisturbed	well developed; no evidence of a plow horizon (Ap)
	pH	4.0–4.5	4.0–4.5
	Drainage/texture	well drained	well drained
	Geologic formations	gneiss, schist, quartz, monzonite, Triassic sandstone, quartzite, and/or conglomerate	quartzite, quartz schist, phyllite
Canopy stress index		no stressors	gypsy moth, chestnut blight historically
Landscape context	Interior patch size	8 ha (20 ac)	total coverage of Dry Oak Forest at Valley Forge NHP: 75 ha (186 ac) and white oak dominated stands: 83 ha (204 ac)
	Circularity index	High	high in the vicinity of Mount Joy and Mount Misery
	Stand area to disturbance patch size ratio	50:1	needs to be determined.
	Home ranges and Dispersal distances	4 ha (10 ac)	total coverage of Dry Oak Forest at Valley Forge NHP: 75 ha (186 ac) and white oak dominated stands: 83 ha (204 ac)
	Surrounding landscape	forested cover with no roads, trails, edges, high connectivity between forest patches	forested in the vicinity of Mount Misery and Mount Joy; minor trails are present; good connectivity between forest patches

DRY-MESIC CHESTNUT OAK FOREST "A" LEVEL CRITERIA

Valley Forge Name: **Dry Oak Forest (Mesic variant)**
NVC Name: *Quercus prinus - Quercus rubra / Hamamelis virginiana* **Forest**
NVC Code: **CEGL006057**

Target Environmental Condition: Sites occupied by this dry-mesic chestnut oak forest are mostly protected rocky mountain slopes. Habitats are underlain by a variety of bedrock types, including metabasalt (greenstone), pyroxene-rich granitic rocks, Antietam and Tuscarora quartzites, metasiltstone and phyllite, shale, and sedimentary material (interbedded sandstone, siltstone, and shale). This community typically occupies lower to middle-slope topographic positions, but can also occur on steep (approximately 27 degrees), usually concave slopes, with relatively high surface cover of outcrops, boulders, and stones. Slope aspect is variable, but in general, aspects range from north to southeast. In Virginia, stands classified as this type, soil samples are strongly to very strongly acidic (mean pH = 4.8) but had moderately high levels of calcium (mean = 1019 ppm), reflecting the frequent occurrence of this community on moderately base-rich substrates (Fleming and Coulling 2001).

Target Vegetation Composition and Structure: The vegetation is usually a closed-canopy forest codominated by chestnut oak and northern red oak in variable proportions. Canopy associates include pignut hickory, mockernut hickory, shagbark hickory, American chestnut, tuliptree, red maple, and blackgum. A tall-shrub layer is occasionally present and usually characterized by flowering dogwood and witch hazel. The lower shrub layer is sometimes dense and ericaceous, with species such as mountain laurel, black huckleberry, and early lowbush blueberry, and also commonly contains mapleleaf viburnum. The herbaceous layer is usually sparse but may include a large number of low-cover species such as wintergreen, whorled yellow loosestrife (*Lysimachia quadrifolia*), New York fern (*Thelypteris noveboracensis*), tall rattlesnake root (*Prenanthes altissima*), variable rosette grass (*Dichanthelium commutatum)*, witchgrass (*Dichanthelium dichotomum*), Pennsylvania sedge, Christmas fern (*Polystichum acrostichoides*), striped pipsissewa, naked-flower tick-trefoil (*Desmodium nudiflorum*), purple bedstraw (*Galium latifolium*), feathery false lily-of-the-valley (*Maianthemum racemosum*), white wood aster (*Eurybia divaricata*), and smooth Solomon's seal (*Polygonatum biflorum*).

Target Dynamics: Wind and ice damage to tree crowns and fire are natural disturbances for this community.

Target Species Composition:

Stratum	Lifeform	Species	Target Cover Range
Tree canopy	Broad-leaved deciduous tree	chestnut oak	20–40%
Tree canopy	Broad-leaved deciduous tree	northern red oak	10–30%
Tree canopy	Broad-leaved deciduous tree	American chestnut	5–15%
Tree canopy	Broad-leaved deciduous tree	pignut hickory	5–15%
Tree canopy	Broad-leaved deciduous tree	shagbark hickory	5–15%
Tree canopy	Broad-leaved deciduous tree	mockernut hickory	5–15%
Tree canopy	Broad-leaved deciduous tree	tuliptree	2–10%
Tree subcanopy	Broad-leaved deciduous tree	red maple	2–10%
Tree subcanopy	Broad-leaved deciduous tree	blackgum	2–10%
Tall shrub	Broad-leaved deciduous tree	flowering dogwood	2–15%
Tall shrub	Broad-leaved deciduous shrub	witch hazel	5–15%
Low shrub	Broad-leaved evergreen shrub	mountain laurel	5–15%
Low shrub	Broad-leaved deciduous shrub	mapleleaf viburnum	5–15%
Low shrub	Broad-leaved deciduous shrub	early lowbush blueberry	20–40%
Low shrub	Broad-leaved deciduous shrub	black huckleberry	30–50%
Low shrub	Broad-leaved evergreen shrub	wintergreen	2–10%
Herb	Fern	Christmas fern	~1%
Herb	Grass	Pennsylvania sedge	~1%
Herb	Forb	whorled yellow loosestrife	~1%
Herb	Forb	white wood aster	~1%
Herb	Forb	smooth Solomon's seal	~1%

SUCCESSIONAL TULIPTREE FOREST: MESOPHYTIC FOREST "A" LEVEL CRITERIA

Unlike the Dry Oak Forest in which the current and target vegetation types are the same and desired condition is a matter of degree, the Successional Tuliptree Forest is in itself an undesired type and requires replacement by a different desired vegetation type. However, there is no currently described NVC equivalent of the target vegetation community for two reasons: a) the NVC describes existing vegetation, and few if any high quality, well documented examples of historic vegetation of this type exists; and b) forests of the northern piedmont are a confluence of different environmental factors, further complicating classification. The most direct relationship is to the Mesic Oak – Beech Forest (NVC type *Fagus grandifolia - Betula lenta - Quercus (alba, rubra) / Carpinus caroliniana* Forest, CEGL006921), a provisional type newly described from Morristown National Historical Park. Rather than attempting to modify an existing provisional description, we base our description of the desired type on historical references and other sources detailed in this report.

Existing Valley Forge Name: **Tuliptree – Oak Forest**
NVC Name: *Liriodendron tulipifera – Quercus velutina* **Forest**
NVC Code: **CEGL007221**

Desired Community Type: Mesophytic Forest

Target Environmental Condition: The desired forest type occurs on slightly alkaline soils including limestone, dolostone, shale, and sandstone as well as occasionally on quartzite on lower slopes where more moisture is available, and on steep north to west facing slopes at low altitudes. In some stands the pH can be as high as 6, but typically is > 4.5) (Kasmer et al. 1984; Keever 1973). The community is also found on level to rolling topography on middle and lower slopes of ridges. It occurs on gneiss, granodiorite, granite gneiss, felsic gneiss, diabase, anorthosite, Wissahichson schists and soils derived from the Stockton and Ledger Formations. The leaf litter layer is well developed, compacted and relatively flat. Soil decomposition rates are rapid and the soil contains relatively high cation concentrations. Pit and mound microtopography is common in these stands, as windstorms uproot canopy trees.

Target Vegetation Structure and Composition: The desired community consists of a mixed canopy of white oak, black oak, northern red oak, American beech and tuliptree. Shagbark hickory (*Carya ovata*), mockernut hickory (*Carya alba = C. tomentosa*), pignut hickory (*Carya glabra*), and American chestnut are also present in the canopy. American basswood may be present in some stands. The subcanopy is dominated by red maple, white ash, American hornbeam (*Carpinus caroliniana*), flowering dogwood, eastern redbud, and occasionally black walnut (*Juglans nigra*). Sugar maple is uncommon in this community, although it may occur in the understory of stands close to the glacial boundary in southeastern Pennsylvania or on more fertile soils. The shrub layer is relatively inconspicuous. Where present, the dominant shrubs are mapleleaf viburnum and /or northern spicebush. A noticeably diverse herbaceous layer is present. Although no one species dominates, the following herbs may be present in variable proportions: bloodroot (*Sanguinaria canadensis*), liverleaf (*Hepatica nobilis*), spring beauty (*Claytonia virginica*), wild ginger (*Asarum canadensis*), Dutchman's breeches (*Dicentra* *cucullaria*), crane's bill (*Geranium maculatum*), sweet cicely (*Osmorrhiza longistylis*), rue anemone (*Anemonella thalictroides*), jack-in-the-pulpit, miterwort (*Mitella diphylla*), false Solomon's seal (*Smilacina racemosa*), meadow-rue (*Thalictrum dioicum*), Solomon's seal (*Polygonatum biflorum*) ebony spleenwort (*Asplenium platyneuron*), rattlesnake fern (*Botrychium virginianum*), Christmas fern, maidenhair fern (*Adiantum pedatum*), wood ferns (*Dryopteris* spp.), mayapple (*Podophyllum peltatum*), blue cohosh (*Caulophyllum thalictroides*), and others.

Target Species Composition:

Stratum	Lifeform	Species	Target Cover Range
Tree canopy	Broad-leaved deciduous tree	white oak	10–25%
Tree canopy	Broad-leaved deciduous tree	black oak	10–25%
Tree canopy	Broad-leaved deciduous tree	northern red oak	10–25%
Tree canopy	Broad-leaved deciduous tree	American beech	10–25%
Tree canopy	Broad-leaved deciduous tree	tuliptree	10–25%
Tree canopy	Broad-leaved deciduous tree	American chestnut	5–10%
Tree canopy	Broad-leaved deciduous tree	shagbark hickory	5–10%
Tree canopy	Broad-leaved deciduous tree	mockernut hickory	5–10%
Tree canopy	Broad-leaved deciduous tree	pignut hickory	5–10%
Tree canopy	Broad-leaved deciduous tree	American basswood	0–5%
Tree subcanopy	Broad-leaved deciduous tree	red maple	10–20%
Tree subcanopy	Broad-leaved deciduous tree	white ash	10–20%
Tree subcanopy	Broad-leaved deciduous tree	American hornbeam	5–10%
Tree subcanopy	Broad-leaved deciduous tree	flowering dogwood	1–5%
Tree subcanopy	Broad-leaved deciduous tree	eastern redbud	1–5%
Tree subcanopy	Broad-leaved deciduous tree	black walnut	0–3%
Low shrub	Broad-leaved deciduous shrub	mapleleaf viburnum	1–5%
Low shrub	Broad-leaved deciduous shrub	northern spicebush	1–5%
Herb	Fern	Christmas fern	~1%
Herb	Forb	wild ginger	~1%
Herb	Forb	bloodroot	~1%
Herb	Forb	liverleaf	~1%
Herb	Forb	smooth Solomon's seal	~1%
Herb	Forb	jack-in-the-pulpit	~1%

Target Dynamics: Fires are infrequent in these stands, thereby maintaining fire intolerant species in the understory and favoring them over oaks. Examples of this community typically occur in geographic areas that are fire breaks such as north-facing slopes and ravines (Overlease 1987). Major (canopy killing) fire intervals are 100–500 years allowing for oak regeneration; however minor periodic fires on mesic sites favor oak expansion (Nowacki 1993). American beech is more common on north facing slopes, while oaks hickories are more common on south facing slopes (Gordon 1941; Harshberger 1919). Windthrow and lightning fire are also common disturbances in this community. Both disturbances open up small canopy gaps and release shade tolerant mesic species. Oaks require larger canopy disturbances for regeneration. A balance of disturbance regimes is required for this community to remain stable.

Reference Sites[9]:

- The Peak Forest, Pennypack Ecological Restoration Trust, Huntington Valley, Montgomery County, PA, referred to as beech-tuliptree-red oak forest by Kershner and Leverett (2004). The Peak Forest is a remnant stand of old woodland located on slopes too steep and rocky to use for agriculture, but undoubtedly logged selectively. Deer and invasive exotic plants are stressors of this stand. American beech and tulip poplar dominate this community along with white ash. Flowering dogwood is very common. Red maple, hickories and oaks are also common in the canopy. Black cherry, blackgum, black walnut, sassafras and American elm are present, but not abundant (Robertson 2006). The soils underlying the Peak Forest are mapped in the Soil Survey of Montgomery County as Manor very stony silt loam and Manor stony land, steep (USDASCS 1967).
- Fort Washington State Park, Montgomery County, PA, referred to as oak-hickory-tuliptree forest by Pearson (1974).
- The Five Mile Woods Preserve in Lower Makefield Township, Bucks County contains a mesic mixed oak - beech forest stand which occurs on the Fall Line between the Bryn Mawr Formation and Bridgeton Formation; an increasing white-tailed deer population is a growing problem (Rhoads 2006).
- Crumb Creek on the campus of Swarthmore College was studied by Harshberger (1904). Crumb woods occurs on Wissahickon Schist; it remains more or less intact with large tuliptrees along with oak and American beech (Rhoads 2006).
- Otter Creek Natural Area, York County, owned by Pennsylvania Power and Light, a remnant stand of a mesophytic ravine community also with umbrella magnolia (Kershner and Leverett 2004).
- Mettler's Woods (Hutcheson Memorial Forest), Rutgers University, NJ, mesophytic oak-hickory forest (Kershner & Leverett 2004).
- Helyar Woods, Rutgers University, NJ, mesophytic oak-hickory forest (Kershner & Leverett 2004).
- Saddler's Woods, Camden County, NJ, American beech-tuliptree-mixed oak-hickory forest (Kershner & Leverett 2004).

Other potential reference sites resemble the desired Mesophtyic forest type, but further study will be required to determine whether these stands should be used as reference sites:

- Wissahickon Valley portion of Fairmount Park (in Philadelphia) has some areas of mature mixed oak and oak - beech forest canopy occurring on Wissahickon Schist; the lower levels of the forest are impacted by an increasing abundance of white-tailed deer and invasives to varying degrees (Rhoads 2006).
- Shenks Ferry ravine within the Lower Susquehanna Valley, a remnant stand of a mature mixed mesophytic community in character occurring on limestone soils with a very diverse herbaceous flora and umbrella magnolia *(Magnolia tripetala)* in the understory and an occasional chinquapin oak *(Quercus muhlenbergii)* (Rhoads 2006).

References: Harshberger 1904; Harshberger 1919, Gordon 1941, Pearson 1963, Kasmer et al. 1984, Keever 1973, Braun 1950; Overlease 1978, Frelich and Reich 1996, Nowacki 1993; Rhoads 2006; Kershner & Leverett 2004.

---

[9] Reference sites for the desired forest type are not necessarily old growth; they include relatively mature stands with relatively few artifical disturbances

Target Ecological Integrity Metrics for Mesophytic Forest "A" Level Criteria

Table 4, at the end of this section, provides a summary of Mesophytic Forest target values or ranges compared to existing Successional Tuliptree Forest conditions at Valley Forge NHP for the following ecological integrity metrics.

Stand Metrics:

Stand Structural Class: An estimated range for target stand density for a mesophytic forest type at Valley Forge NHP is 208 trees/ha (83 trees/ac) to 380 trees/ ha (150 trees/ac) (trees >10 cm dbh) and an estimated target range for stand basal area is 40 m^2/ha (172 ft^2/ac) to 120 m^2/ha (530 ft^2/ac) (Runkle 1996; Gaines et al. 1997; Runkle 2000; Robertson 2006). This community has moderate to high species richness and diversity in the canopy. White oak, northern red oak, American beech, and tuliptree are the most important canopy tree species. The structure of the stand is multi-layered and multi-aged with most tree species in the canopy and subcanopy. Disturbance regimes influence these stand metrics. For example, fire will increase the amount of oak, decrease the cover of mesic species, and open the understory; while windthrow will open a small canopy gap that favors shade-tolerant advanced regeneration (Frelich and Reich 2002). Identifying an exact range of stand density and basal area criteria for the desired conditions requires further sampling of old-growth mesophytic stands in the Piedmont Uplands. Likewise, site-specific conditions such as slope position, aspect, substrate, and geographical position in the landscape (i.e. firebreak, adjacent to a watercourse, slope, ridge, etc.) will also influence the structure of the community (Frelich and Reich 2002). An estimated average target seedling density for these stands is 10,000 seedlings/ha (4,000 seedlings/ac) and an estimated average target sapling density is 3,000 saplings/ha (1,200 saplings/ac) (Overlease 1978).

Canopy Closure: A desired canopy closure for a high quality example of this community is 87–99% (Monk 1957 in Gaines et al. 1997). Small gaps created by windthrow favor advanced regeneration shade-tolerant species; while larger canopy gaps favor oak regeneration.

Snag Abundance: The desired snag abundance for this community ranges from 15–20 snags/ha, ≥25 cm dbh, and ≥2.5 m high (6–10 snags/ac, ≥10 in dbh, and ≥8.2 ft tall) (Runkle 1996, 2000). There are snags of multiple ages and size classes in various stages of decay based on past disturbances in the forest (McCarthy 2003). Snag abundance is a variable metric driven by various disturbances and may be higher or lower depending on time since disturbance (White and White 1996).

Coarse Woody Debris (CWD): The desired amount of CWD in this community is 25–50 tons/ha (10–20 tons/ac) with an average of 15 downed logs/ha (6 logs/ac) ≥30 cm (11 in) mid-diameter (Runkle 1996; Lang and Forman 1978 in Gaines et al.1997). The amount of CWD may vary based on the intensity of past disturbances, the types of disturbance, and time since last disturbance. However, in general, there will be a considerable presence of downed logs of multiple age and decay classes.

Photopoint: Potentially representative or related plots at VAFO from vegetation mapping and classification project: VAFO.58, VAFO.50, VAFO.16 and VAFO.75 (understory composition) (Podniesinski et al 2005).

Tree Metrics:

Tree Condition: Trees should be of large diameter, with robust trees near maximum size and age for the species and site. Proposed diameter sizes for the largest trees in Valley Forge old-growth mesophytic forests include white oak: 182–243 cm (6–8 ft); American beech: 122 cm (4 ft); tuliptree: 182 cm (6 ft); and hickories: 30–60 cm (1–2 ft) (Harshberger 1904; Runkle 1996; Gaines et al. 1997). The desired age of the trees in this community is ≥200 years (Frei and Fairbrothers 1963 in Gaines et al. 1997).

Tree growth and mortality rates: Trees in this community exhibit slow growth rates. A target average annual basal area increase for each species ranges from 3–5%, while the target overall stand basal area remains constant from year to year. Annual stand density increases from 0–0.5% per year and decreases as basal area increases (Runkle 2000). Targeted growth rates slow and taper off to zero after the stand is dominated by few, large-diameter trees. A target mortality rate is averaged approximately 1%/year. Mortality rate is related to stem size; greater in the smallest subcanopy stems (<20 cm) and the largest-sized canopy stems (>50 cm) than in mid-sized stems (20–50 cm dbh) (Runkle 2000). Mortality is also sporadic and disturbance driven from windthrow, lightning fires, ice storms, and occasional canopy fires. Growth rates are species specific.

Tree regeneration: Tree seedlings and saplings of the canopy trees are present in these old-growth stands, but not necessarily abundant. The amount of regeneration is disturbance driven. An estimated average target seedling density for these stands is 10,000 seedlings/ha (4,000 seedlings/ac) and an estimated average target sapling density is 3,000 saplings/ha (1,200 saplings/ac) (Overlease 1978). Small canopy openings favor mesic species regeneration and large canopy openings favor oak regeneration. There is considerably more advanced regeneration of shade-tolerant mesic species such as American beech and maple than oak seedlings and saplings.

Understory Metrics:

Indicator Plants- American beech, white oak, and northern red oak are characteristic trees, eastern redbud a characteristic shrub, and bloodroot, round lobe hepatica, and other slow colonizing mesic forest herbs are characteristic of this community. The shrub layer is inconspicuous and the herbaceous layer is noticeably diverse and conspicuous.

The local ephemeral flora can be used to help estimate the ecological integrity of a desired Mesophytic Forest. McCarthy (2003) provides examples of ephemeral species, including Canada wild ginger, narrowleaf spring beauty, Carolina crane's-bill, round-lobe hepatica, bloodroot, trilliums, and others. This author suggests that six or more ephemeral species and other old-growth criteria indicate high quality old growth; 2–5 ephemeral species indicate intermediate integrity; and <2 ephemeral species indicate lower quality. Additional indicator species of old-growth mesophytic forests should be identified in addition to ephemeral species. The herbaceous layer is the most diverse vegetation layer in mesophytic old-growth stands. As a result, when sampling them, three sampling seasons per year are needed to capture 95% of the herb species (McCarthy 2003).

Exotic plants: An absence of exotic invasive plants is a desired condition. Invasive species may be prevalent in successional stages of this community; however, they should decline over time with elimination of stressors such as excessive deer browse as the stand matures. Increased shade conditions favor native herbs adapted to these conditions as "old growth herb layers exhibit all three forms of stability: resistance, resilience and persistence" (McCarthy 2003).

Understory diversity: A diverse native herbaceous layer comprised of shade-tolerant mesophytic species is a diagnostic indicator of this community. Species richness of native herbs will increase as stands mature, and level off as competition for resources in the understory increase with advanced regeneration tree species (McCarthy 2003). Herb species richness is associated with pit and mound microtopography. The shrub layer consists of native species and is relatively sparse.

Soil metrics:

Forest Floor Composition: The forest floor should be a thick organic layer with soil macropores. Pits and mounds are formed by individual tree mortality from windthrow, lightning fire, or old age which results in an uprooted tree. The resulting pit and mound microtopography is typical in these stands, which increases spatial heterogeneity throughout the forest floor.

Soil chemistry: The diversity of the herbaceous layer is related to soil fertility and soil moisture regime (Gilliam and Roberts 2003). Soil chemistry varies, however, soils typically have higher pH values—up to 6.9 with high concentrations of calcium (>560 ppm), magnesium (0.45 ppm), and potassium >50 ppm) (Keever 1973; Kasmer et al. 1984). American beech is the dominant canopy tree in areas where the soils have higher phosphorous values, on north-facing slopes, and on soils with a pH range from 3.8–4.4. Oaks are more dominant on south-facing slopes with dry, acidic soils (pH of 4) and lower cation concentrations values (Kasmer et al. 1984).

Landscape Metrics:

Landscape context: Old-growth Mesophytic Forests require sufficient area to provide propagule sources for slow-growing ancient forest-adapted herbs. Stands must also be large enough to support old-growth patch dynamics (White and White 1996). Stand shape should minimize edge; a recommended ratio of stand area to disturbance patch size is 50:1 to ensure optimal regeneration (White and White 1996). The minimal interior patch size is 8 ha (20 ac), but larger stands (ten ha or more) are recommended to support characteristic fauna, to support dispersal among patches, and to reduce edge effect. The desired shape of the patch is circular and wide, rather than linear, to maintain the core old-growth forest conditions. Desired conditions also include connectivity to other mesophytic stands, as well as minimal fragmentation, to maintain community structure and provide close proximity to seed sources for slow-colonizing forest herbs (Verheyen et al. 2003). The land adjacent to the stand should be forested to minimize edge and limit invasion of exotic species from open fields.

Table 4. Summary of target ecological integrity metrics compared to existing forest conditions (where measured or known) for Valley Forge National Historical Park Successional Tuliptree Forests.

Metric	Sub metric	Estimated Target Ranges for Old-growth Mesophytic Forest Community	Existing Conditions for Valley Forge NHP Successional Tuliptree Community
Stand structural class	Overstory Basal Area	40 m2/ha (172 ft2/ac) to 120 m2/ha (530 ft2/ac)	As the desired community is a completely different community type from the existing community, the comparison of metrics and conditions is limited. Available data was not specific to the Successional Tuliptree community.
	Tree density (trees >10 cm dbh)	208 trees/ha (83 trees/ac) to 380 trees/ha (150 trees/ac) (trees >10 cm dbh)	
	Age	Canopy trees >200 years old multiple age classes	~100 years old
	Structure	multiple structural classes	Tuliptree dominant; many stands lack tall and short shrub stratum (Figure 4)
Canopy closure		87–99%	~85%
Snag abundance		15–20 snags/ha >25 cm dbh and >2.5 m high (6–10 snags/ac >10 in dbh and >8.2 ft tall)	needs to be determined
Coarse woody debris		25–50 tons/ha (10–20 tons/ac) with an average of 15 downed logs/ha (6 logs/ac) >30 cm (11 in) mid-diameter	needs to be determined
Tree condition	Overall	large diameter, healthy robust trees with spreading crowns	Oak mortality from 1980s gypsy moth epidemic, but good canopy recovery from disturbance; American chestnut no longer in canopy from blight
	DBH estimates for largest trees	white oak: 182–243 cm (6 to 8 ft); American beech: 122 cm (4 ft); tuliptree: 182 cm (6 ft); and hickories: 30–60 cm (1–2 ft)	Need to analyze Plots data more closely, but average Successional Tuliptree community diameters were 40 cm (16 in) dbh and ranged from 14–90 cm (6–35 in) dbh
Tree growth and mortality rates	Age	Canopy trees >200 years old multiple age classes	80–100 years
	Net annual growth	average annual basal area increase for each species ranges from 3–5%; target overall stand basal area remains constant from year to year. Annual stand density increases from 0–0.5%/year, and decreases as basal area increases	greater than zero
	Mortality rate	1%/year.	Undetermined
Tree regeneration	Sapling density	3,000 saplings/ha (1,200 saplings/ac)	These metrics need to be determined. Data from Bowersox and Larrick (1999) may be related, but not community specific for direct comparison
	Seedling density	10,000 seedlings/ha (4,000 seedlings/ac)	
	Stressors	None	deer browse, exotics, lack of stand regenerating disturbance regime

Table 4. Summary of target ecological integrity metrics compared to existing forest conditions (where measured or known) for Valley Forge National Historical Park Successional Tuliptree Forests (continued).

Metric	Sub metric	Estimated Target Ranges for Old-growth Mesophytic Forest Community	Existing Conditions for Valley Forge NHP Successional Tuliptree Community
Indicator plants		beech, white oak, northern red oak, eastern redbud, bloodroot, and round lobe hepatica and other slow colonizing mesic forest herbs	tuliptree
Exotic plants		Zero	garlic mustard and Japanese stiltgrass dominant herbs
Understory diversity	Species richness	moderate to high	moderate to high
	Dominant species	bloodroot, and round lobe hepatica and other slow colonizing mesic forest herbs	Flowering dogwood, Japanese stiltgrass, garlic mustard
Forest floor condition	Leaf litter layer	thick organic layer with soil macropores	thick, well developed
	Microtopography	pit and mound characteristic	pit and mound uncharacteristic
Soil chemistry	Soil history-landuse	forested; not converted to agriculture	Sites cleared for agriculture, fields for encampment, settlement, some stands planted
	Soil profile	well developed and undisturbed	well developed; Ap most likely present
	pH	Wide range site specific 3.8–6.9, but typically >4.5	4.0–4.5?
	Drainage/texture	moderately well drained	well drained
	Geologic formations	gneiss, granodiorite, granite gneiss, felsic gneiss, diabase, anorthosite, Wissahickon schists and soils derived from the Stockton and Ledger Formations	Triassic Stockton (sandstone, siltstone) and Cambrian Ledger Formations (dolomite), Cambrian Antietam and Harpers Formations (quartz, phyllite, schist),
Canopy stress index		no stressors	gypsy moth, chestnut blight historically
Landscape context	Interior patch size	8 ha (20 ac)	total coverage of Successional Tuliptree Forest at Valley Forge NHP: 151 ha (374 ac), but stands are relatively fragmented
	Circularity index	High	low
	Stand area to disturbance patch size ratio	50:1	needs to be determined.
	Home ranges and Dispersal distances	4 ha (10 ac)	total coverage of Successional Tuliptree Forest at Valley Forge NHP: 151 ha (374 ac), but stands are relatively fragmented
	Surrounding landscape	forested cover with no roads, trails, edges, high connectivity between forest patches	low connectivity between patches; many stands adjacent to fields and roads

Discussion

The purpose of this report is to identify a set of possible desired conditions for the existing Dry Oak and Successional Tuliptree forest communities at Valley Forge NHP. The target communities and conditions selected were based on those that, to the best of our knowledge, existed on the Valley Forge NHP landscape at the time of early European settlement and through the Revolutionary War Encampment. As the mission of Valley Forge NHP is to commemorate the encampment period, it was appropriate to select forest communities that may have occurred on the landscape during that time period

Management Implications for Valley Forge National Historical Park

The existing Dry Oak Forest community at Valley Forge NHP is relatively intact and is on a trajectory to eventually reach the target conditions discussed in this report, provided some adaptive management actions are taken. The key components of this community requiring correction are the lack of a stand-maintaining disturbance regime and lack of oak regeneration in the understory. As in many forests of the northeast, the absence of a once prominent canopy tree, the American chestnut, is notable. Consideration should be given to participating in a wider American chestnut reintroduction program in the coming years.

Similar ecological stressors exist in the Valley Forge NHP Successional Tuliptree stands. Although exotic species are also present in the Dry Oak Forest, they pose a substantial additional stress in the Successsional Tuliptree Forest. These stands in no way resemble the desired community type in structure, composition, or function, and will require intensive adaptive management to realign them towards the desired historical Mesophytic community described in this report.

Recommendations for Future Projects

An initial attempt to qualitatively assess the ecological integrity of the Valley Forge NHP forests was made. However, as it was beyond the scope of this project, it is highly recommended that ecological integrity assessments be completed to document baseline conditions. Additional field studies at the identified examples of old-growth Dry Oak and Mesophytic forests are recommended to provide more quantitative data. Ecological integrity of the existing Valley Forge NHP forests can be compared to old-growth stands through the application of the forest monitoring protocol methods used in this report (Tierney and Faber-Langendoen 2005).

Additional witness tree research should be completed for towns near Valley Forge NHP and within Chester County to provide more time-specific data on forest composition during the early colonial period (1680–1800). Historic documents including letters, journals, and plans may reveal more information about the forested portions of the landscape at the time of encampment and prior to encampment.

Continued sampling of the deer exclosure plots is recommended to provide insight into the future composition of the forest communities in the absence of a deer browse disturbance regime. A study examining the soil seed banks within both communities is also recommended.

Conclusions

This report identifies an approach to quantifying desired forest conditions. Once final target conditions are identified for the Valley Forge NHP Dry Oak and Successional Tuliptree forest communities, ecological integrity assessments can be completed and stand metrics generated for comparison to target conditions. By using the NVC to identify desired condition and linking desired condition to an ecological integrity framework, the methods discussed in this report can help translate forest monitoring results into management decisions.

The descriptions and metrics detailed in this report characterize the highest quality ("A" level) stands, or those stands that exhibit the greatest ecological integrity when compared to stands that existed historically. Given the current stressors on the forests of Valley Forge NHP such as invasive exotics, small patch size, substantial deer browse, interruption of natural disturbance regimes, and the surrounding urban landscape setting, we recognize that "A" level stands are essentially not achievable. Development of interim, or lower quality but acceptable criteria should be developed, using the provided "A" level criteria as a guide. Additional study will be required to determine whether pursuing restoration by implementing lower-ranked criteria at Valley Forge will result in forests that are viable over the long term. If the decision is made to pursue forest restoration at the park, criteria can be modified and adjusted as the forests are monitored and more is learned about their structure, composition, and dynamics. Realigning the existing forests on a trajectory towards a desired condition will take explicit, well-defined management goals, significant resources, and commitment to long-term forest management.

Literature Cited

Abrams, M. D. 1992. Fire and the development of oak forests. Bioscience 42:346–353.

Abrams, M. D. 2002. The postglacial history of oak forests in eastern North America. *In* Oak Forest Ecosystems. Eds. W. J. McShea and W. M. Healy. The Johns Hopkins University Press. Pp 34–45.

Abrams, M. D. 2003. Where has all the white oak gone? BioScience 53(10):927–939.

Abrams, M. D., D. A. Orwig, and T. E. Demeo. 1995. Dendroecological analysis of successional dynamics for a presettlement-origin white-pine-mixed oak forest in the southern Appalachians, USA. Journal of Ecology 83:123–133.

Abrams, M. D., and G. J. Nowacki. 1992. Historical variation in fire, oak recruitment, and post-logging accelerated succession in central Pennsylvania. Bulletin of the Torrey Botanical Club 119:19–28.

Bellemare, J., G. Motzkin, and D. R. Foster. 2003. Legacies of the agricultural past in the forested present: an assessment of historical land-use effects on rich mesic forests. Journal of Biogeography 29:1,401–1,420.

Black, B. A., and M. D. Abrams. 2001. Influences of Native Americans and surveyor biases on metes and bounds witness tree distribution. Ecology 82:2,574–2,586.

Bowersox, T. W., and D. S. Larrick. 1999. Long-term vegetation monitoring of forested ecosystems at Hopewell Furnace National Historic Site and Valley Forge National Historical Park. Technical Report NPS/PHSO/NRTR-99/077. USDI National Park Service. Mid-Atlantic Region. Philadelphia, PA. 68 pp.

Braun, E. L. 1950. Deciduous Forests of Eastern North America. Blackburn Press. Caldwell, NJ. 576 pp.

Brown, S. L., and P. E. Schroeder. 1999. Spatial Patterns of Aboveground Production and Mortality of Woody Biomass for Eastern U.S. Forests. Ecological Applications 9:968–980.

Buell, M. F., A. N. Langford, D. W. Davidson, and L.F. Ohmann. 1966. The upland forest continuum in Northern New Jersey. Ecology 32:416–432.

Cypher, B. L., R. H. Yahner, and E. A. Cypher. 1985. Ecology and management of white-tailed deer at Valley Forge National Historical Park. Mid-Atlantic Regional Office. National Park Service. U. S. Department of the Interior. 245 pp.

Daeschler, E., E. E. Spamer, and D. C. Parris. 1993. Review and new data on the Port Kennedy local fauna and flora (Late Irvingtonian), Valley Forge National Historical Park, Montgomery County, Pennsylvania. *The Mosasaur* 5:23–41.

Davis, C., J. Comiskey, K. Callahan. 2006. MidAtlantic Park Profiles. Appendix 2. National Park Service. Mid-Atlantic Inventory & Monitoring Network. www.nature.nps.gov/im/units/midn/Phase_1_Report/Appendix_2._Park_Profiles.pdf.

Davis, M. A., J. Pergl, A. Truscott, J. Kollmann, J. P. Bakker, R. Domenech, K Prach, A. Prieur Richard, R. M. Veeneklaase, P. Pysek, R. del Morali, and others. 2004. Vegetation change: a reunifying concept in plant ecology. Perspectives in Plant Ecology. Evolution and Systematics 7:69–76.

deCalesta, D. S. 1997. Deer and ecosystem management. Pages 267–279 in McShea, W. J., H. B. Underwood, and J. H. Rappole, eds. The Science of Overabundance. Smithsonian Institution Press. Washington, DC.

Dey, D. 2002. Fire history and postsettlement disturbance. In Oak Forest Ecosystems. Eds., W. J. McShea and W. M. Healy. The John Hopkins University Press. Pp. 46–59.

Fleming, G. P., and P. P. Coulling. 2001. Ecological communities of the George Washington and Jefferson national forests, Virginia. Preliminary classification and description of vegetation types. Virginia Department of Conservation and Recreation, Division of Natural Heritage. Richmond, VA. 317 pp.

Foster, D. R., S. Clayden, D. A. Orwig, B. Hall and S. Barry. 2002. Oak, American chestnut and fire: climactic controls of long-term forest dynamics in New England, USA. Journal of Biogeography 29:1359–1279.

Frelich, L. E., and P. B. Reich. 2002. Dynamics of old growth oak forests in the eastern United States. In Oak Forest Ecosystems. Eds., W. J. McShea and W. M. Healy. The Johns Hopkins University Press. Pp. 113–128.

Gaines, G., P. Arndt, S. Croy, M. Devall, C. Greenburg, S. Hooks, B. Martin, S. Neal, G. Pierson, and D. Wilson. 1997. Guidance for conserving and restoring old-growth forest communities on National Forests in the Southern Region. Report of the Region 8 Old-Growth Team. 117 pp.

Gawler, S. 2002. Analysis of Valley Forge NHP 1998 deer exclosure data for any insights into the Vegetation types, for NVC Mapping. Unpublished-file notes. NatureServe. Boston, MA.

Gilliam, F. S., and M. R. Roberts. 2003. Interactions between the herbaceous layer and overstory canopy of eastern forests. In The Herbaceous Layer in Forests of Eastern North America. Eds. F. S.Gilliam and M. R. Roberts. Oxford University Press. New York, NY. Pp. 198–223.

Gordon, R. B. 1941. The natural vegetation of West Goshen Township, Chester County, PA. Pennsylvania Academy of Science 15:194–199.

Harshberger, J. W. 1904. A phyto-geographic sketch of extreme southeastern Pennsylvania. Bulletin of the Torrey Botanical Club 31(3):125–159.

Harshberger, J. W. 1919. Slope exposure and the distribution of plants in eastern Pennsylvania. Geographical Survey of Philadelphia Bulletin 17:53–61.

Heister, K. M., G. W. Fairchild, and A. M. Faulds. 2002. Analysis of understory vegetation in fenced and unfenced plots at Valley Forge National Historical Park, 1993–1998. Final Report. U. S. Department of Interior, National Park Service, Valley Forge National Historical Park.

Kasmer, J., P. Kasmer, and S. Ware. 1984. Edaphic factors and vegetation in the Piedmont Lowland of southeastern Pennsylvania. Castanea 49:147–157.

Keever, C. 1973. Distribution of major forest species in southeastern Pennsylvania. Ecological Monographs 43:303–327.

Kershner, B., and R. T. Leverett. 2004. The Sierra Club Guide to the Ancient Forests of the Northeast. Sierra Club Books. San Francisco, CA. 276 pp.

Keys, J. E., Jr., C. A. Carpenter, S. L. Hooks, F. G. Koenig, W. H. McNab, W. E. Russell, M. Smith. 1995. Ecological Units of the Eastern United States, First Approximation. 1:3,500,000 map and accompanying map unit tables. USDA Forest Service.

Kuchler, A. W. 1964. Potential natural vegetation of the conterminous United States. American Geographical Society. Special Publication No. 36. New York, NY.

Lindenmayer, D. B., and J. F. Franklin. 2002. Conserving forest biodiversity: a comprehensive multiscaled approach. Island Press. Washington, DC. 351 pp.

McCabe, T. R., and R. E. McCabe. 1997. Recounting whitetails past. Pages 11–26 in W. J. McShea, H. B. Underwood, and J. H. Rappole, eds. The Science of Overabundance: Deer Ecology and Population Management. Smithsonian Institution Press. Washington DC.

McCarthy, B. C. 2003. The herbaceous layer of eastern old growth deciduous forests. In The Herbaceous Layer in Forests of Eastern North America. Eds., F. S. Gilliam and M. R. Roberts. Oxford University Press. New York, NY. Pp. 163–176.

Mikan, C. J., D. A. Orwig, and M. D. Abrams. 1994. Age structure and successional dynamics of a presettlement-origin Chestnut oak forest in the Pennsylvania Piedmont. Bulletin of the Torrey Botanical Club 121:13–23.

National Park Service (NPS). 2001. NPS Management Policies. Page 28.

Nerurkar, J. D. 1974. Plant communities on a quartzite ridge in Chester County, Pennsylvania. Proceedings of the Pennsylvania Academy of Science 48:101–106.

Nowacki, G. J. 1993. Final project report: the development of old-growth definitions for the Eastern United States, Phase II [Unpublished report]. On file with: 1720 Peachtree Rd, Atlanta, GA 30367. USDA, Forest Service, Southern Region. 218 pp.

Overlease, W. R. 1978. A study of forest communities in southern Chester County, Pennsylvania. Proceedings of the Pennnsylvania Academy of Science 52:37–44.

Overlease, W. R. 1987. 150 years of vegetation change in Chester County, Pennsylvania. Bartonia 53:1–12.

Paillet, F. L. 2002. American chestnut: History and ecology of a transformed species. Journal of Biogeography 29:1,517–1,530.

Pearson, P. R., Jr. 1963. Vegetation of a woodland near Philadelphia. Bulletin of the Torrey Botanical Club 90:171–177.

Pearson, P. R., Jr. 1974. Woodland vegetation of Fort Washington State Park, Pennsylvania. Bulletin of the Torrey Botanical Club 101:101–104.

Pennsylvania Geological Survey. 1981. Map 61,591: Valley Forge Quadrangle. Atlas of Preliminary Geologic Quadrangle Maps of Pennsylvania. Pennsylvania Geological Survey.

Pennsylvania Geological Survey. 1993. Pennsylvania Trail of Geology Valley Forge National Historical Park: The Geologic History. Commonwealth of Pennsylvania. 13 pp.

Pennsylvania Bureau of Topographic and Geographic Survey. 2001. Bedrock Geology of Pennsylvania: shape-file format, Reading 30'x 60' quadrangle. Pennsylvania Bureau of Topographic and Geographic Survey, DCNR.

Petergill, R. 1924. Letter from America 1776–1779: Being letters of Brunswick, Hessain and Waldick officers with the British Army during the Revolution. Kennikat Press, Inc. Prt Washington, NY.

Podniesinski. G. S., L. A. Sneddon, J. Lundgren, H. Devine, B. Slocumb, and F. Koch. 2005. Vegetation classification and mapping of Valley Forge National Historical Park. Technical Report NPS/NER/NRTR—2005/028. National Park Service. Philadelphia, PA.

Rhoads, A. F., and T. A. Block. 2004. The Trees of Pennsylvania A Complete Reference Guide. University of Pennsylvania Press.

Rhoads, A. F., D. Ryan, and E. W. Aderman. 1989. Land use study of Valley Forge National Historical Park. Final Report. U.S. Department of Interior, National Park Service, Valley Forge National Historical Park. Contract #: CA4000-7-8021.

Roberts, M. R., and F. S. Gilliam. 2003. Response of the herbaceous layer to disturbance in eastern forests. Herbaceous Layer in Forests of Eastern North America. Eds., F. S. Gilliam and M. R. Roberts. Oxford University Press. New York, NY. Pp. 302–320.

Runkle, J. R. 1996. Central mesophytic forests. *In* Eastern Old Growth Forests. Ed., M. B. Davis. Island Press. Washington DC. Pp. 161–177.

Runkle, J. R. 2000. Canopy tree turnover in old-growth mesic forests of eastern North America. Ecology 81(2):554–567.

Russell, E. W. B., and A. E. Schuyler. 1988. Vegetation and flora of Hopewell Furnace National Historic Site, eastern Pennsylvania. Bartonia 54:124–143.

Shreve, F. 1910. Ecological plant geography of Maryland, Mountain Zone. In Plant Life of Maryland. The John Hopkins Press. Pp. 275–292.

Southeast Exotic Pest Plant Council. 2005. Invasive plants of the eastern United States. www.invasive.org/eastern/eppc/japgrass.html (accessed November 2006).

Tierney, G., and D. Faber-Langendoen. 2005. Draft NETN forest protocol. Northeast Temperate Network. National Park Service. 93 pp.

Trombulack, S. C. 1996. The restoration of old growth: Why and How. In Eastern Old Growth Forests. Ed., M. B. Davis. Island Press. Washington DC. Pp. 305–320.

United States Department of Agriculture Soil Conservation Service (USDA SCS). 1967. Soil Survey Montgomery County Pennsylvania. The Pennsylvania State University and Pennsylvania Department of Agriculture.

Unknown (maybe Burns, F.). 1901. A Sectional Bird Census. Taken at Berwyn, Chester County, Pennsylvania, During Seasons of 1899. 1900 and 1901.

Valley Forge National Historical Park (VAFO). 2006. Valley Forge NHP DRAFT General Management Plan / Environmental Impact Statement. PA.

Verheyen, K., O. Honnay, G. Motzkin, and D. R. Foster. 2003. Response of forest plant species to land-use change: a life-history trait-based approach. Journal of Ecology 91:563–577.

Watts, W. A. 1979. Late Quaternary vegetation of the central Appalachians and the New Jersey coastal plan. Ecological Monographs 49:427–469.

Wayne, I. 1814. Isaac Wayne, Esq., on Timber at Valley Forge. Pages 376–377 in Memoirs of the Philadelphia Society for Promoting Agriculture Containing Communications on Various Subjects in Husbandry and Rural Affairs, Vol. III. Johnson and Warner. Philadelphia, PA.

Whitbeck, M. 1995. Accumulation of fallen woody debris in old growth stands of western Massachusetts: A search for a definition of old growth. 11 pp.

White, P. S., and R. D. White. 1996. Old growth Oak and Oak-Hickory Forests. In Eastern Old Growth Forests. Ed., M. B. Davis. Island Press. Washington, DC. Pp. 178–198.

Wisconsin DNR. 2001. Community restoration and old growth on the Northern Highland – American Legion State Forest. Wisconsin Department of Natural Resources. Publication Number: PUB-FR-139b 2001.

Appendix A. NatureServe Ecological Classifications Glossary of Terms.

alluvial - characterized by the deposition of sediment by a stream or other running water at any point along its course.

alpine - the zone on mountain tops between permanent snow and the cold limits of trees.

annual - plant species that complete their life-cycle within a single growing season.

annual vegetation - associations that persist for less than one year or are dominated by annual species.

biennial - plant species that complete their life-cycles within two growing seasons.

Boreal - northern biogeographical region typically referring to subpolar and cold temperate areas.

Brackish - tidal water with a salinity of 0.5–30 parts / thousand.

broad-leaved - describes a plant with leaves that have well-defined leaf blades and are relatively wide in outline (shape) as opposed to needle-like or linear; leaf area is typically greater than 500 square millimeters or 1 square inch.

bryophyte - nonvascular, terrestrial green plant, including mosses, hornworts, and liverworts.

bunch grass - multi-stemmed (caespitose) life form of grasses characterized by clumps of erect shoots that slowly spread horizontally by tillers, generally creating distinct individual plants spaced across the ground; often applied to sedges and other graminoids with similar life forms.

caespitose (cespitose) - describes a low branching pattern from near the base that forms a multistemmed or a bunched appearance.

cliff - any high, very steep to perpendicular, or overhanging face of a rock outcrop.

cloud forest - tropical and subtropical montane forest characterized by a high incidence of low-level cloud cover, usually at the canopy level, promoting development of an abundance of vascular epiphytes.

cold-deciduous - describes a plant that sheds its leaves as a strategy to avoid seasonal periods of low temperature, often initiated by photoperiod; applied to vegetation adapted to seasonal cold season influences (temperate).

conical-crowned - describes a needle-leaved evergreen tree with a pyramidal or cone-shaped canopy or life form; for example, Douglas fir and silver fir (*Pseudotsuga menziesii* and *Abies amabilis*).

creeping - describes the pattern of stems growing at or just beneath the surface of the ground and usually producing roots at nodes.

crustose lichen - lichen life form that grows in intimate contact with its substrate, lacks a lower cortex and rhizoids (root-like structures), and is impossible to separate from the substrate without destroying the thallus; lichen with an unlobed, flattened thallus, growing adnate to the substrate.

cushion plant - a low, woody, plant life form so densely branched that it forms a compact canopy that is pad- or bolster-like in appearance; usually with microphyllous foliage; characteristic of alpine and tundra plants.

cylindrical-crowned - describes a needle-leaved evergreen tree with a narrow, essentially cylinder-shaped canopy or life form; for example, subalpine fir and black spruce (*Abies lasiocarpa* and *Picea mariana*).

deciduous - describes a woody plant that seasonally loses all of its leaves and becomes temporarily bare-stemmed.

deciduous vegetation - associations in which deciduous woody plants generally contribute 75% or more to total dominant plant cover.

dominant - an organism, group of organisms, or taxon that by its size, abundance, or coverage exerts considerable influence upon an association's biotic (such as structure and function) and abiotic (such as shade and relative humidity) conditions.

drought-deciduous - describes a plant that sheds its leaves as a strategy to avoid seasonal periods of high transpiration demand; applied to vegetation adapted to climates with seasonal drought and little cold-season influence (tropical-subtropical).

dwarf-shrub - low-growing shrub life form usually under 0.5 meter or 1.5 feet tall (never exceeding 1 meter or 3 feet tall) at maturity.

dwarf-shrubland - vegetation dominated by low-growing shrubs, usually under 0.5 m or 1.5 feet tall; dwarf-shrubs generally form greater than 25% cover, and trees and taller shrubs generally form less than 25% cover. Dwarf-shrub cover may be less than 25% where it exceeds tree, shrub, herb, and nonvascular cover.

ECS - abbreviation for NatureServe's eastern region (formerly "Eastern Conservation Science").

ephemeral forb vegetation - annual associations or synusiae that, during favorable periods, dominate areas that are usually sparsely vegetated or unvegetated for most of the year.

epiphyte - vascular plant that grows by germinating and rooting on other plants or other perched structures; sometimes called "air plants."

episodic forb vegetation - herbaceous-dominated associations that occupy areas periodically denuded of vegetation.

ericaceous or ericoid - plants of the Heath Family or Family Eriaceae; for example, heaths, rhododendrons, and blueberries (*Erica*, *Rhododendron*, and *Vaccinium*).

evergreen - describes a plant that has green leaves all year round; or a plant that in xeric habitats has green stems or trunks and never produces leaves.

evergreen vegetation - associations in which evergreen woody plants generally contribute 75% or more to total dominant plant cover; vegetation canopy is never without photosynthetic tissue.

extremely xeromorphic - associations that are adapted primarily to growing in drought-persistent environments and are only secondarily adapted to other environmental stresses; plants typically have several well-developed xeromorphic characteristics.

facultatively deciduous - describes evergreen species that shed leaves only under extreme conditions; this strategy is often associated with plants found in semiarid saline/alkaline environments; for example, *Atriplex-Kochia* saltbush in Australia and North America.

foliose lichen - lichen life form that is leafy in appearance and loosely attached to its substrate; lichen with a lobed, flattened thallus growing loosely attached to the substrate, the lobes flattened or inflated with distinctly differentiated upper and lower surfaces; umbilicate lichens are included.

forb - a broad-leaved herbaceous plant.

forest - vegetation dominated by trees with their crowns overlapping, generally forming 60 – 100% cover; includes reproductive stages or immature secondary growth stands that are temporarily less than 5 meters or 16.5 feet tall.

fresh water - water with a salinity of less than 0.5 parts / thousand.

fruticose lichen - lichen life form that is bunched, shrubby or "hairy" in appearance and loosely attached to its substrate; lichen with the thallus branched, the branches solid, or hollow and round, or flattened without distinctly differentiated upper and lower surfaces; squamulose lichens are included.

GC 1. - an abbreviation for "global classification" indicating a standard type accepted into the ICEC (compare with "OC"). 2. a global rank indicating that the type is planted or cultivated (see global rank).

giant - describes mature forests in which the height of a typical canopy exceeds 50 meters or 165 feet.

global rank (G Rank) - conservation status rank for natural/near-natural communities:

GX   **ELIMINATED** throughout its range, with no restoration potential due to extinction of dominant or characteristic species.

GH   **PRESUMED ELIMINATED (HISTORIC)** throughout its range, with no or virtually no likelihood that it will be rediscovered, but with the potential for restoration (e.g., *Castanea dentata* Forest).

G1   **CRITICALLY IMPERILED** Generally 5 or fewer occurrences and/or very few remaining acres or very vulnerable to elimination throughout its range due to other factor(s).

G2   **IMPERILED** Generally 6–20 occurrences and/or few remaining acres or very vulnerable to elimination throughout its range due to other factor(s).

G3   **VULNERABLE** Generally 21–100 occurrences. Either very rare and local throughout its range or found locally, even abundantly, within a restricted range or vulnerable to elimination throughout its range due to specific factors.

G4   **APPARENTLY SECURE** Uncommon, but not rare (although it may be quite rare in parts of its range, especially at the periphery). Apparently not vulnerable in most of its range.

G5   **SECURE** Common, widespread, and abundant (though it may be quite rare in parts of its range, especially at the periphery). Not vulnerable in most of its range.

GU   **UNRANKABLE** Status cannot be determined at this time.

G?   **UNRANKED** Status has not yet been assessed.

Modifiers and Rank Ranges

?   A question mark added to a rank expresses an uncertainty about the rank in the range of 1 either way on the 1–5 scale. For example a G2? rank indicates that the rank is thought to be a G2, but could be a G1 or a G3.

G#G#   Greater uncertainty about a rank is expressed by indicating the full range of ranks which may be appropriate. For example, a G1G3 rank indicates the rank could be a G1, G2, or a G3.

Q   A "Q" added to a rank denotes questionable taxonomy. It modifies the degree of imperilment and is *only* used in cases where the type would have a *less imperiled* rank if it were not recognized as a valid type (i.e., if it were combined with a more common type). A GUQ rank often indicates that the type is unrankable *because of* daunting taxonomic/definitional questions.

Ranks indicating semi-natural/altered communities:

GD   **RUDERAL** Vegetation resulting from succession following anthropogenic disturbance of an area. Generally characterized by unnatural combinations of species (primarily native species, though often containing slight to substantial numbers and amounts of species alien to the region as well).

GM   **MODIFIED/MANAGED** Vegetation resulting from the management or modification of natural/near natural vegetation, but producing a structural and floristic combination not clearly known to have a natural analogue.

GW   **INVASIVE** Vegetation dominated by invasive alien species; the vegetation is spontaneous, self-perpetuating, and is not the (immediate) result of planting, cultivation, or human maintenance.

Rank indicating planted/cultivated communities

GC   **PLANTED/CULTIVATED** Areas dominated by vegetation that has been planted in its current location by humans and/or is treated with annual tillage, a modified conservation tillage, or other intensive management or manipulation.

graminoid - grasses and grass-like plants, including sedges and rushes.

G Rank - see global rank.

grassland - vegetation dominated by perennial graminoid plants.

growth form - the shape or appearance of a plant; primarily a reflection of the influence of growing conditions.

hemi-sclerophyllous - describes a plant with stiff, firm, leathery leaves that partially retain their rigidity during wilting; for example, rhodendron and salal (*Rhododendron* and *Gaultheria*).

herb - a vascular plant without significant woody tissue above or at the ground; an annual, biennial, or perennial plant lacking significant thickening by secondary woody growth, with perennating buds borne at or below the ground surface (hemicryophytes, geophytes, helophytes, and therophytes of Raunkier).

herbaceous vegetation - vegetation in which herbs (graminoids, forbs, and ferns) are dominant; herbs generally form at least 25% cover while trees, shrubs, and dwarf-shrubs generally form less than 25% cover. Herb cover may be less than 25% where it exceeds tree, shrub, dwarf-shrub, and nonvascular cover.

hygromorphous herbs - herbaceous plants structurally adapted for life in water-dominated or aquatic habitats.

intermittently flooded - substrate is usually exposed, but surface water can be present for variable periods without detectable seasonal periodicity. Inundation is not predictable to a given season and is dependent upon highly localized rain storms. This modifier was developed for use in the arid West for water regimes of Playa lakes, intermittent streams, and dry washes but can be used in other parts of the U.S. where appropriate. This modifier can be applied to both wetland and non-wetland situations. *Equivalent to Cowardin's Intermittently Flooded modifier.*

irregularly exposed - land surface is exposed by tides less often than daily; the area from mean low tide to extreme low spring tide. *Equivalent to Cowardin's Irregularly Exposed modifier.*

irregularly flooded - tidal water floods land surface less often than daily. The area must be flooded by tides at least once yearly as a result of extreme high spring tide plus wind plus flow. The area extends from mean high water inland to the maximum extent of tide plus the splash zone. *Equivalent to Cowardin's Irregularly Flooded modifier*, except in tidal Riverine, Lacustrine, and Palustrine areas where if an area is only irregularly flooded by fresh tidal waters, the appropriate non-tidal modifier, e.g., Temporarily Flooded, Seasonally Flooded, Semipermanently Flooded, applies.

krummholz - growth form assumed by tree species at the upper treeline or in the alpine zone; characterized by a creeping and multi-stemmed growth pattern due to desiccation and physical damage caused by wind and blowing ice crystals near the upper treeline; the same species grows as an erect, single-stemmed tree at lower elevation.

LACD - abbreviation for NatureServe's Latin American and Caribbean region.

lichen - an organism generally recognized as a single plant that consists of a fungus and an alga or cyanobacterium living in symbiotic association.

lignified - describes a plant with woody tissue developed by secondary cell wall thickening by lignin and cellulose.

life form - the shape or appearance of a plant that mostly reflects inherited or genetic influences.

low forb - a broad-leaved herbaceous plant usually less than 1 meter or 3 feet tall when inflorescences are fully developed.

lowland - a large land area with vegetation reflecting limits set by regional climate and soil/site conditions; an area where elevation is not the primary gradient affecting vegetation zonation.

matted - describes a creeping plant that by reiterative growth has overlapping stems and forms a low, dense ground cover.

MCS - abbreviation for NatureServe's midwestern region (formerly "Midwest Conservation Science").

medium-tall grassland - graminoid-dominated vegetation usually between 0.5 to 1 meter or 1.5 to 3 feet tall when inflorescences are fully developed in temperate zones and to 2 meters or 6 feet in tropical zones.

microphyllous - describes a plant with small leaves; individual leaf surface areas are less than 500 square millimeters or one square inch.

mixed evergreen-deciduous - describes vegetation in which evergreen and deciduous species each generally contribute 25–75% to the total canopy cover.

montane - describes the zone in mountainous regions where the influence of altitude (vertical relief) results in local climatic regimes that are sufficiently different from those in the adjacent lowlands as to cause a complex vertical climate-vegetation-soil zonation; includes vegetation at the base of a mountain when it is different from lowland vegetation.

natural/semi-natural - describes vegetation that has not been planted or treated with an annual management or manipulation regime.

needle-leaved - describes a plant with slender, elongated leaves; for example, pine and fir trees (*Pinus* and *Abies*).

nonvascular plant - a plant without specialized water or fluid conductive tissue (xylem and phloem); includes bryophytes, non-crustose lichens, and algae.

nonvascular vegetation - vegetation that is dominated by nonvascular plants (bryophytes, non-crustose lichens, and algae), generally forming at least 25% cover, with other vegetation forming less than 25 percent cover. Nonvascular cover may be less than 25% where it exceeds tree, shrub, dwarf-shrub, and herb cover.

OC - an abbreviation for "other classification" indicating a type that is not part of the ICEC, but is a state or local type, a non-terrestrial type, or any other type not accepted into the ICEC.

pavement - a relatively flat surface of consolidated material, generally exposed bedrock.

perennial - plant species with a life-cycle that characteristically lasts more than two growing seasons and persists for several years.

perennial herbaceous vegetation - associations that persist for several years and are dominated by herbaceous species.

permanently flooded - water covers the land surface at all times of the year in all years. Equivalent to Cowardin's "permanently flooded".

permanently flooded-tidal - salt water covers the land surface at all times of the year in all years. This modifier applies only to permanently flooded areas irregularly flooded by fresh tidal water. Equivalent to Cowardin's "permanently flooded/tidal".

planted/cultivated - describes vegetation planted by humans and/or treated with annual management; usually dominated by plants not indigenous to the area.

polar - geographically, the areas within the Arctic and Antarctic circles in which the sun is entirely not visible for six months and is constantly above the horizon for the next six months; climatically, polar regions are characterized by the lack of a period of warmth and by enduring cold; in polar climates the average temperature of each month is below 10° C (50° F).

pulvinate mosses - mosses growing in cushion-like mats or clumps.

rainforest - vegetation in frost-free areas dominated by trees that are always wet from rain.

regularly flooded - tidal water alternately floods and exposes the land surface daily, from mean low (lower low on West Coast) to mean high (higher high on West Coast). *Equivalent to Cowardin's Regularly Flooded modifier.*

revolute - rolled toward the lower surface of a leaf.

rosulate - a plant with leaves arranged in rosettes (circular clusters).

rounded-crowned - describes a needle-leaved evergreen tree with a basically semi-circular canopy or life form; for example, whitebark pine and alligator juniper (*Pinus albicaulis* and *Juniperus deppeana*).

saltwater - water with a salinity of greater than 30 parts / thousand.

saturated - surface water is seldom present, but substrate is saturated to surface for extended periods during the growing season. *Equivalent to Cowardin's Saturated modifier.*

scale-leaved - describes a plant with small, overlapping leaves that usually lie flat on the stem; for example, eastern redcedar and western redcedar (*Juniperus virginiana* and *Thuja plicata*).

sclerophyllous - describes a plant with usually evergreen leaves that are stiff and firm and retain their stiffness even when wilted; they are common in, but not restricted to, regions with a long summer drought and predictable yet limited winter rain.

scree - a sheet of coarse rock debris covering a mountain slope without an adjacent cliff.

scrub - vegetation dominated by shrubs, including thickets. See shrubland.

SCS - abbreviation for NatureServe's southeastern region (formerly "Southeast Conservation Science).

seasonal - showing periodicity related to the seasons; applied to vegetation exhibiting pronounced seasonal periodicity marked by conspicuous physiognomic changes.

seasonal evergreen vegetation - associations in which most of the up/ canopy plants retain leaves year-round and drop some leaves during unfavorable seasons.

seasonally flooded - surface water is present for extended periods during the growing season, but is absent by the end of the growing season in most years. The water table after flooding ceases is very variable, extending from saturated to a water table well below the ground surface. *Includes Cowardin's Seasonal, Seasonal-Saturated, and Seasonal-Well Drained modifiers.*

semi-arid - a climatic region having an annual precipitation, usually between 25.4 and 50.8 centimeters or 10 and 20 inches, that is higher than a truly arid climate; typically, vegetation is composed of grasses with or without woody plant layers.

semi-deciduous vegetation - associations (usually tropical and subtropical) in which most of the up/ canopy trees are drought-deciduous and many of the understory trees and shrubs are evergreen. The evergreen and deciduous woody plants are not always separated by layers.

semi-evergreen vegetation - associations in which evergreen and deciduous species each generally contribute 25–75% of total tree cover; specifically, this term refers to tropical and subtropical vegetation in which most of the up/ canopy trees are evergreen mixed with drought-deciduous trees.

semipermanently flooded - surface water persists throughout growing season in most years except during periods of drought. Land surface is normally saturated when water level drops below soil surface. *Includes Cowardin's Intermittently Exposed and Semipermanently Flooded modifiers.*

short grassland - graminoid-dominated vegetation usually less than 0.5 meters or 1.5 feet tall when inflorescences are fully developed.

shrub - a perennial woody species with a life form that is usually less than 4 to 5 meters or 13 to 16 feet in height; typically, plants have several stems arising from or near the ground, but this term includes short tuft-tree, bamboo, and woody vine species; length of vine may exceed 5 meters; shrub species growth form may be taller than 5 meters or single-stemmed under certain environmental conditions.

shrubland - vegetation dominated by shrubs, generally greater than 0.5 meter or 1.5 feet tall and less than 5 meters or 16 feet tall, and generally forming greater than 25% cover; trees generally form less than 25% cover. Shrub cover may be less than 25% where it exceeds tree, dwarf-shrub, herb, and nonvascular cover. Includes vegetation dominated by woody vines; does not include developing secondary associations dominated by tree species.

sod grass - a life form of graminoids that tends to develop a solid mat of grass, sedge, etc. over the ground by vegetative increase of rhizomes or stolons; resulting vegetation generally has few spaces between plants.

sparse vegetation/sparsely vegetated - describes vegetation with low total plant cover. Abiotic substrate features are dominant; vegetation is scattered to nearly absent and generally restricted to areas of concentrated resources. Total vegetation cover is typically less than 25% and greater than 0%. Areas with high cover of crustose lichen and no other vegetation are included here.

stomata - pores or openings for gas exchange that are generally concentrated on leaf surfaces.

subalpine - upper mountain vegetation immediately below the cold limits of tree and tall shrub growth.

subdesert - an area of xerophytic shrubby vegetation with a poorly-developed herbaceous layer.

submontane - an area where the influence of altitude (vertical relief) does not result in local climate regimes that are sufficiently different from the adjacent lowlands as to cause a complex vegetation-climate-soil zonation; generally includes the foothills of a mountain range; the lowland vegetation at the base of a mountain that displays vegetation zonation.

subpolar - geographically, the region immediately equatorward of the Arctic and Antarctic circles; climatically, winters are long and extremely cold, and summers are very short; only one month / year has a monthly average warmer than 10° C (50° F); as a rule, the ground is completely covered by snow for at least half a year; the region between the tundra and cold temperate forests or steppes.

subtropical - pertains to areas within tropical regions with variable (seasonal) temperature and moisture regimes; climatically, it has seasonal variation marked by dry/wet seasons rather than cold/hot seasons; parts of this region are subject to sub-0° C (32° F) temperatures but rarely have freezing periods of 24 hours or longer; in the United States this term includes southern Florida and the southern tip of Texas.

succulent - a plant with fleshy stems or leaves with specialized tissue for the conservation of water; a xeromorphic strategy for tolerating long periods of drought.

suffruticose - a somewhat shrubby plant in which the upper vegetative and flowering shoots die back to leave only the lower parts to survive unfavorable seasons.

synusia - an association of plant species with a similar life form and similar ecological requirements occurring together in the same habitat; sometimes called a "union"; most habitats are occupied by several synusiae, which may grow above each other in layers, beside each other, or in mixture; for example, an open tree synusia or layer over a grass-dominated synusia or layer.

tall grassland - graminoid-dominated vegetation usually over 1 meter or 3 feet tall when inflorescences are fully developed in temperate zones and greater than 2 meters or 6 feet in tropical zones.

tall forb - broad-leaved herbaceous plants usually greater than 1 meter or 3 feet tall when inflorescences are fully developed.

talus - a sloping accumulation of coarse rock fragments at the base of a cliff.

temperate - geographically, the region between the polar and tropical regions; climatically, the region is moderate with distinct seasons of alternating long, warm summers and short, cold winters.

temporarily flooded - surface water present for brief periods during growing season, but water table usually lies well below soil surface. Often characterizes flood-plain wetlands. Equivalent to Cowardin's Temporary modifier.

tidally flooded - flooded by the alternate rise and fall of the surface of oceans, seas, and the bays, rivers, etc. connected to them, caused by the attraction of the moon and sun [or by the back-up of water caused by unfavorable winds].

tree - perennial, woody species life form with a single stem (trunk), normally greater than 4 to 5 meters or 13 to 16 feet in height; under certain environmental conditions, some tree species may develop a multi-stemmed or short growth form (less than 4 meters or 13 feet in height).

treeline - a zone where the normal growth of trees is limited; cold temperatures often combined with drought form the upper or arctic treeline, and drought combined with hot temperaturesform lower or arid treeline.

tropical - geographically, the area between the Tropic of Cancer (23 27' N) and the Tropic of Capricorn (23 27' S), which includes tropical montane and alpine zones; climatically, the tropics are described as either the equatorial limits of freeze or, in temperate marine locations without freezing, the 65° F isotherm for the coldest month of the year; generally, tropical regions are characterized by high mean temperatures, small annual variation in temperature, and abundant rainfall throughout the year, although mountainous areas within the tropics are more variable.

tuft-tree - woody plant with large leaf-fronds or rosulate branches at the tips of major trunk(s); for example, palms and tree ferns.

tundra - the treeless region north of the Arctic Circle (arctic tundra) or above the treeline of high mountains (alpine tundra) and on some sub-Antarctic islands; characterized by very low winter tempatures, short cool summers, permafrost below a surface layer subject to summer melt, short growing season, and low precipitation.

tussock - graminoid life form consisting of bunch-like tufts, sometimes more than 1 meter or 3 feet tall, in which the hard, old, withered leaves are intermingled with the fresh, young, green leaves.

vascular plant - a plant with water and fluid conductive tissue (xylem and phloem); includes seed plants, ferns, and fern allies.

woodland - vegetation dominated by open stands of trees with crowns not usually touching (generally forming 25–60% cover); canopy tree cover may be less than 25% in cases where it exceeds shrub, dwarf-shrub, herb, and nonvascular cover, respectively.

woody - containing lignified plant tissue.

woody plant - plant species life form with woody tissue and buds on that woody tissue near or at the ground surface or above; plants with limited to extensive thickening by secondary woody growth and with perennating buds; includes phanerophytes and chamaephytes of Raunkier.

xeromorphic - describes plants with morphological and physiological characters that tolerate persistently low water availability, such as succulence, specialized leaf surfaces for light reflectance or water retention, opportunistic leaf growth, leaf-size reduction with increased thickness and sunken stomata, revolute margins, or stem and leaf modification to form thorns or spines.

Appendix B. Draft Forest Condition Monitoring Protocol and Metrics (from Tierney and Faber-Langendoen 2005).

	Metric	Objectives	Vital Sign(s)
		Specific objectives of the Northeast Temperate Network Forest Protocol	
Standard metric	Stand structural class	Determine the distribution of structural classes and determine change over time. Compare the distribution of structural classes to that expected under natural disturbance regimes.	Forest vegetation
	Canopy closur	Determine if canopy closure is decreasing over time. Examine relationships between canopy closure and climatic stress, storms, pest and pathogen outbreaks and other disturbances.	Forest vegetation
	Snag abundance	Estimate snag abundance and determine change over time. Examine whether land management is reducing snag.	Forest vegetation
	Coarse woody debris (CWD)	Estimate coarse woody debris biomass or volume. Determine if CWD is increasing or stable. Examine whether land management and silviculture are reducing CWD.	Forest vegetation
	Photopoint	Provide visual reference of plots for long-term qualitative comparison.	Forest vegetation
Tree metrics	Tree condition	Qualitatively assess tree condition and determine if condition of any tree species is declining over time.	Forest vegetation, Exotic animals – early detection
	Tree growth and mortality rates	Estimate growth and mortality rates by tree species. Determine if growth rates are declining or if mortality rates are increasing over time. Examine correlation between vital rates and air pollution, pest or pathogen outbreaks, climatic stress or other known stressors.	Forest vegetation
	Tree regeneration	Quantify canopy tree seedlings and saplings by species and size class. Determine if tree regeneration is increasing or decreasing over time. Determine species composition of tree regeneration.	Forest vegetation, White-tailed deer herbivory
Understory metrics	Indicator plants	Determine the spatial extent of high priority invasive exotic plant species and track changes over time. Determine population trends of species most palatable to deer, most sensitive to ozone and acid deposition, or at the southern or lower edge of their range.	Forest vegetation, Exotic plants – early detection, White-tailed deer herbivory, Acid deposition & stress, Ozone
	Understory diversity	Estimate native understory plant species richness and determine if richness is declining over time. Determine if exotic plant species are increasing in abundance.	Forest vegetation, Exotic plants – early detection
Soil metrics	Forest floor condition	Qualitatively assess forest floor condition. Determine the spatial extent of invasive exotic earthworms, a well-developed humus layer, and trampling impacts. Determine change over time.	Forest vegetation, Visitor usage, Exotic animals – early detection
	Soil chemistry	Determine soil Ca:Al an C:N ratios to assess the extent to which base cation depletion, increased aluminum availability and/or nitrogen saturation are impacting NETN forest soils. Determine whether the impact is increasing over time.	Forest vegetation, Acidic deposition & stress
	Canopy stress index	Determine the extent and magnitude of canopy stress within NETN forested systems from remotely sensed red reflectance data. Examine correlation between stress and covariates including air pollution exposure, pest and pathogen outbreaks, climatic stress and other known stressors.	Forest vegetation, Acidic deposition & stress, Ozone
	Landscape context	Assess landscape context impacting plot. Determine interior patch size. Determine distance from plot to roads, trails, and other anthropogenic edges. Determine proportion of surrounding area in natural cover and in anthropogenic landuse. Determine change over time.	forest vegetation, Landcover, Landue

NPS D-094 March 2007